EDGING GOD OUT

Richard J. Hart

PublishAmerica
Baltimore

First printing

Softcover 9781462696512
PUBLISHED BY PUBLISHAMERICA, LLLP
www.publishamerica.com
Baltimore

Printed in the United States of America

Dedication: To all my friends for their support and prayers

Table of Contents

INTRODUCTION

Edging God Out is the title selected to introduce this collection of thoughts which describe the struggles every human being undergoes within his or her ego, that is the attitude of self esteem, self importance, or inflated sense of self worth. *Edging God Out* is reduced to the word "ego" and represents the very act of putting one's self in God's place. All forms of egoism whether psychological, ethical or rational maximize one's own welfare or self interest, satisfying one's own desires or getting what one wants. Altruism is the opposite of egoism, a characteristic which we should strive to have. We edge God out by being blind to the realities around us. Like Bartimaeus, we need to ask Jesus that we may see with new eyes and persist in asking as he did. We need a wide angled lens to see what needs to be done so as not to fall into a pall of forgetfulness. We grow spiritually when we see everything aflame with Divine Fire. The worst of times can become the best of times when seen through the lens of the cross. Do we look at life with glazed eyes or blurred vision? Do we have the tensile strength to see how important it is not to mask our disinterest or hide behind a sense of privacy?

We edge God out of our lives by not listening to God speaking to us by staying below the radar screen. Or we listen to the wrong advice, especially when bombarded by consumerism and materialism to "buy, buy and pay later." God can speak to us like Elijah in a gentle whisper. Jesus truly listened to what the Father wanted him to do especially in the garden. Some forty to sixty percent of our day is spent in listening. How much do we actively listen or give our undivided attention, especially when surrounded by so much noise? We place roadblocks or obstacles to listening by being judgmental, being in control of others, not being silent. Listening to our own bodies and feelings can be very challenging because we often ignore them.

People definitely edge God out of their lives when they sexually abuse others, especially children. Loving, tender, touching can have a wholesome effect on our lives and the lives of others. Jesus touched many people during his life time: Jairus' daughter, Peter's mother-in-law, lepers, Peter sinking in the water. He was also touched by others: the woman with the hemorrhage, the sinful woman, Mary Magdalene. The early Church continued to make use of the power of touch; recall Peter and John in the temple curing the lame man, Ananias with Saul, laying on of hands by the Apostles. We need to continue to reach out to the outcasts of our society--people with the HIV virus, AIDS, prostitutes, homeless, people with disabilities, immigrants and many others.

We might congratulate ourselves on being loving people. But is our love as unconditional as God's who woos us into knowing how much we are loved. Jesus gave us a radical challenge when he said that we are to "love our enemies, do good to those who hate us, pray for those who mistreat us." How many of us carry out that command? We find marvelous examples of outstanding love in the Hebrew Scriptures, with the mother of the Maccabees and her sons, Eleazar, and Judith. Jesus showed the highest love by fulfilling what he said, that "no one has greater love than to lay down one's life for one's friend." Forgiveness, an expression of love, is the key which unlocks much of our anger, resentment and revenge. Agape love can transform our lives as it did the lives of many saintly people. Heaven will help us to understand what the highest love is, one that will never end. All that is not love will be burned away.

One of our gifts often taken for granted is our ability to speak. But, marvelous as the gift is, we can abuse it by lying, detraction, slander, backbiting, gossip, unjust anger, taking cheap shots at each other. These abuses lure us into the orbit of toxicity. We need to discipline our thoughts because they are the springboard for our words and actions. We want to avoid being long on jargon and short on deliverables. Some words can burn like hot peppers in our mouths. St. James reminds us how difficult it is to tame our tongue. We need to say good things about others as Paul encouraged his communities, not reveling in the foibles of others. Jesus sets the pace for us by his compassion and care for others.

Justice issues such as the environment, global decisions, fair treatment of all races, cultures, and classes, protecting our ecosystems, climate change, solar energy, enforcing the three R's--reduce, reuse, and recycle, are indeed thorny issues that need attention. If not, we certainly are edging God out of our lives. People like Ashley Judd, Patrick Carolan and many others are devoted to these issues. People power, caused by civil unrest, has certainly exerted itself throughout the world. War will always lead to disaster and is not the answer to our problems. What is needed is greater respect and acceptance of all races, creeds and cultures. The savage cruelty of Trafficking is still rampant abroad and in the United States. Because these lightning rod issues can be overwhelming at times, we need a good sense of humor to deal with them lest we become discouraged. It is most important to develop a spirituality that spurs us on for systemic change, not just for helping us to cope.

As a result of the prevalence of these thorny issues, we often ask the question, "What can I do?" The most ordinary things are drenched in divine possibility. Much needs to be done in our society and throughout the world or the rays of hope will start thinning. Too often we throw in the towel and give up rather than roll up our sleeves and pitch in and rely on our tensile strength. Many examples of people who generously responded to others' needs can also inspire us to do likewise. They did not give into their ego and resist or make excuses, but their acts of goodness transformed the lives of others and their own. Leymah Gbowee, a Liberian peace activist, is convinced that all of us have been created with something unique to contribute.

Fear can easily paralyze us, preventing us from helping others. We can fall into the very errors we decry. Many have a fear of the sacrament of reconciliation. We use all kinds of excuses not to avail ourselves of this wonderful sacrament which has brought so much healing, peace and joy into people's lives. St. John assures us that perfect love will cast out all fear. Too often we airbrush the need from our collective memory. Fear can prevent us from forgiving others and ourselves. Jesus showed us how to forgive others especially through his forgiveness of Judas, Peter, Mary Magdalene. We also have the inspiration of lay people like the Amish. The possibility of failure can also paralyze us because we are not willing to take risks. The thought of dying has paralyzed many because they will do anything to escape this reality. We need to face the question, "What does it mean to die before we die?"

The easiest temptation to give into is to avoid praying. Paul, a spirited Apostle, encouraged people to pray always. Spirited prayer will enable us to counteract any neglect to pray, our distractions, our whirlpool of activities or the siren lure of daily demands, our dryness or spiritual aridity which many saints suffered. We sometimes fill our minds with wistful collages of unfinished business. Our commitment has to become bone deep, not a notional assent. It can become a balm of Gilead to heal us. Spirited prayer will help us to pray away our feelings of anger, resentment, jealousy and sexual feelings. Above all, spirited prayer will transform our lives making a real difference in our lives. Through spirited prayer we find the magnet in our lives enabling us to reach out to the hungry, the poor, the lonely.

CHAPTER ONE
SEEING WITH DIFFERENT EYES

When we were born, we had no knowledge of ourselves; we became aware of others because of our eyes and other senses that open outward. We became conscious first of our mothers and gradually of our own bodies. If we were loved, kissed, hugged, our ego was born. But we still did not know who we were, only what others thought of us. So we formed a false ego if we were rejected, not appreciated, not coddled. The ego became an accumulation of living with others. Everyone reflected to us who we were--family members, teachers, other children, friends. We often do not see how society or others help form our ego either as a true self or a false self. The false self is like a plastic flower; it might be beautiful but it is dead. We have a flowering within, our center, the true self which Hindus call a "lotus," a flower that never stops, never dies. This is what we need to develop. The true self is the person I am before God and the person that I am meant to be.

An image that the writer, Thomas Merton, used to illustrate the false self was that of a mummy wrapped in bandages. Once Francis of Assisi found his true self, he saw how necessary it was to give away all his clothing to his father and stand before others in his nakedness. Merton's change into his true self was gradual when he no longer recognized or saw the man he formerly had written about in *The Seven Story Mountain.* These two men realized how they had edged God out of their lives. They realized the dark reservoirs of their own egotism.

Some years ago I had the opportunity of going to the Holy Land with a group of priests. One of the highlights of that visit was to go to the old city in Jerusalem. It has several gates leading into the city, but one of the main gates is called the Damascus Gate. There are steps leading down into the city before you arrive at the Damascus Gate. On each one of these steps a beggar sat pleading for money. When you look closely at these beggars, you notice that they are blind. Every time that I read or hear the story of Bartimaeus, I am reminded of those blind beggars. Bartimaeus can teach us much about what it means to see, because many of us are often blind to so many realities around us because of the false self or ego. Bartimaeus never saw Jesus but he believed that he could do something for him, and that was to help him to see. He wanted something definite from Jesus. It is important for us to know what we want from Jesus, and to request something very definite. Too often we ask for something rather vague, like we want to be a better Christian, Catholic, father, mother, single person, young adult, or teenager.

We need to ask for something definite like Bartimaeus did or like the leper who asked to be cleansed. There might be a communication problem in marriage which needs healing, and we say "We need to talk." Or some find they are envious and jealous of certain people because of their possessions or talents. Still others might need to pray to let go of feelings of rejection or the treatment received from parents who were cruel to them. There might be some addiction caused by the false ego like overeating, drinking, drugs, smoking which needs healing. We often don't see how we love these pleasures more than we value good health or seek to work out our eternal destiny. Robert Barron believes that egotism has crept into our blood, bones and institutions.

It is very evident from the Gospels that many people wanted to be cured by Jesus. One fifth of the Gospels is taken up with the healing ministry of Jesus. According to Morton Kelsey, Jesus seemed to believe that a primary cause of sickness was a force of evil loose in the world which was hostile to God's way - "edging God out." This is also true today. And Jesus asks us also, as he asked of Bartimaeus, "What do you want?" What do you want from Jesus? Maybe you have to respond like Bartimaeus, "That I may see with different eyes."

Bartimaeus persisted in his request. People were scolding him and telling him in effect, "Shut up." But nothing could stop or silence him. Do we too readily give up or are silenced by others or especially by our false ego? How often do we find ourselves discouraged and say that I can't accomplish this task, or I am unable to accept a challenge. We have to learn not to give up so easily. Toward the end of his life, Beethoven became deaf. He didn't say to God, "How do you expect me to write any music when I am deaf?" He wrote some of his most beautiful music when he was deaf and could not hear it. Milton, toward the end of his life, became blind; he could have lashed out at God and complained, "How do you expect me to write any poetry when I am blind?" He wrote some of his most beautiful poetry when he was blind. Or consider Thomas Edison. It took him some ten thousand experiments before he finally discovered the electric light bulb. Someone asked him one day, "Don't you look upon those experiments as useless?" He responded, "They proved to me what would not work." What a beautiful attitude. So much in life depends on our attitude. The first time Douglas MacArthur applied for admission to West Point, he was turned down. He tried a second time with similar results. Only after his third attempt was he finally accepted and went on to become an outstanding General. Sarah Bernhardt, a famous actress, needed to have her leg amputated at the age of 70, but she continued to act for the next eight years. Albert Einstein claimed that his conclusions took him months, years. He said that 99 times they were wrong, but the 100th time right. Jim Henry was able to conquer his illiteracy in his mid-90's. Then he went on to self-publish *In a Fisherman's Language,* recounting in 29 stories his life. The first two printings sold out, and he advised to never, never give up even if it seems impossible. These individuals and many others never gave up or gave into their false egos.

We might go through life with a negative attitude, always looking at the dark side of life, which the ego will encourage.

Or we feel insignificant like a piece of sand on the whole seashore of life. No wonder we become so easily disheartened and discouraged. We have so many God-given talents and abilities to share with others, and yet often don't use our tremendous potential. Experts point out that we if use 20 percent of our potential, that is extraordinary. Anthropologists say that if we use ten to fifteen percent of our brain power, that is above average. Imagine, then, the untapped potential within everyone of us. But we need to tattoo into our memories that it is not our aptitude or talent, but our attitude that will determine our altitude in life. Many are gifted, but their attitude leaves much to be desired. Do I see the world as nasty, petty, uncivil and gossipy?"The false ego does, but the true self sees a loving, compassionate, forgiving world. Do I see a violent or peaceful world? What am I doing to build a more peaceful and forgiving society?

Peace builders see a different world, one where we can live together in harmony. We need to keep our eye focused on our spiritual radar screen which alerts us to the needs of others.

A Zen master once said, "No seed ever sees the flower." Our challenge is to begin things but maybe not see their fruition. We have seen how Vatican II has brought new life to ancient wineskins. We are an evolving people in an evolving Church. We also see how erosion has begun by those who want to return to the "good old days." We need to continue to see, not with blurred eyes of pessimism, but with wide angled lens how we are the people of God on a march to spread the Good News of the Gospel.

GROWTH IN SEEING

Jesus told us "The lamp of the body is the eye. If your eye is sound, your whole body will be filled with light, but if your eye is bad, your whole body will be in darkness"(Mt.6:22). Meister Eckhart said "The eye with which you see God is the eye with which God sees you."[1] Jesus in many of his parables and sayings, short circuits our wiring and catapults us into another way of seeing. We have to learn how to see well the beauty around us, especially in each other, a task which might take us a life time. We will never see God, but we see the person in front of us who remains a mystery to us until we reach out to the individual. How can we see God's face in others if we don't see the faces they already possess?

Richard Rohr believes that in the second half of our lives we become more aware of events and really see or grasp their meaning. He also maintains that the false self consists in what we think we are. As T.S. Eliot writes, we often have many experiences, but we don't really see or miss their meaning. What is the saying, "experience is what you get when you don't get what you want?" Rohr insists that, "Spiritual maturity is largely a growth in seeing; and full seeing seems to take most of our lifetime, with a huge leap in the final years, months, weeks, days of life, as any hospice volunteer will tell you."[2] The amber lights have been flashing alerts and meaningful messages to us, but our ego helps us to ignore them rather than see them.

Dr. David Liepert, in *Muslim, Christian And Jew*, states that every religion claims that it is good. If that were true, he asks, "Don't you think we'd be seeing some positive results by now? We're not: around the world, arguments and conflicts rage just as they always have. Our planet remains an awfully dangerous place for the most part, religion seems responsible for much of the bloodshed, and it may even be getting worse."[3]

Brother David Steindl Rast, however, maintains that we have to see everything aflame with divine fire. Then we are seeing with the true self. To accomplish that we need to move beyond the visible as well as the invisible barriers we erect and see with the "eyes of our heart." Like Moses we need to remove our shoes to witness the burning bush which did not burn itself up. How do we see or imagine this event? A peak or aha experience might give us a glimpse. Moses came in contact with the burning bush while tending his sheep. That was his peak experience. Ours might come when we are doing some ordinary task which enables us to see with the "eyes of our heart." One person who wanted to see a vision was told to get up and see the sun rise because that is as good as it gets.

Gertrude Stein was an outstanding skillful student at John Hopkins University. The University was ready to award her an M.D. because of her amazing competence in dissecting cadavers. The degree, however, was not given because the University found out about her attitude toward human beings. She did not have the slightest interest or see the need to treat living patients.

Jesus' secret of relating to so many people was his positive attitude toward them. He accepted others as they were, not as he wanted them to become. Jesus did not point out to Zacchaeus what a terrible sinner he was, but invited him to dine with him so he could get in contact with the small man's true self. He encouraged people not to give up and showed us the way better than any GPS. Jesus fell many times under the weight of the cross, not just three times as depicted in the stations of the cross. But each time he got up. We have to learn to rise once more than we fall and that will assure of us of eventual victory. It will also prevent us from becoming discouraged with life and its harsh realities as our ego tempts us to do. We cannot see because the false ego causes its own darkness. The worst of times can become the best of times when seen through the lens of the cross.

Carrying the cross is not for the faint of heart, but it is much easier cheering from a distance. We don't give suffering short shrift. We are sometimes squeezed between our finitude and brokenness. We wish that we were dealt another hand or could reshuffle the cards. At those times we have to embrace our cross, not fleeing into fantasy land or raising a white flag of surrender. The true self sees the vast difference between a heart broken open and a heart broken down. The poet Theodore Roethke believed that in our darkest moments or setbacks our eyes begin to see. We cannot see because the ego causes its own darkness. When we feel miserable, we need to close our eyes and ask what is the cause? The cause is not outside ourselves but from within. When we suffer, the ego is often the cause because it finds reasons for suffering.

Too often we think of "Blessed are the clean of heart, for they will see God," as referring to being virtuous, chaste or celibate. Rather it means being enlightened in heart, single minded as far as righteousness is concerned. Robert Barron believes that we will be happy when there is no ambiguity in our lives or what he calls the deepest center of self, that which is most important to us. It is a matter of cleaning our lens of perception and then we "will see God," and our neighbor. Recall how one criminal did not see who Jesus was and said to him, "Save yourself and us." The other, however, knew Jesus and rebuked the other criminal, saying, "We have been condemned justly." Jesus assured him, "Today you will be with me in Paradise" (Lk 23: 39-43). What a remarkable insight this thief had, one that did not go unrewarded. The Church is always God hung between two thieves.

We often don't see or understand the darkness or evil around us and wonder where God is. We feel that darkness has been cut loose from its moorings. Darkness comes without being announced or invited. But without it we cannot become the persons we are meant to be. By not accepting it, we make matters worse which the false ego endeavors to accomplish. We cannot make all darkness light; complaining about the darkness we empower or deepen it. The tension will continue just like the parable of the weeds and wheat. Evil, according to St. Thomas Aquinas, is nothing, the absence of good. But good will eventually prevail; this is message of Christ's death and resurrection. St. John in his Gospel states, "The light shines in the darkness, and the darkness has not overcome it"(1:5).

Scott Smiley, on patrol in Iraq, remembers a bomb that was set off, sending shards of metal through his eyes and brain. He, as well as others, did not think he would live. In fact, he did not want to live, and he lost his trust in God. Scott was awarded the purple heart and, after grueling physical therapy, convinced his superiors that he had much to contribute. Smiley taught leadership classes at West Point, and having received an MBA from Duke University, now helps wounded and ailing veterans. Scott might not be able to see with his own eyes, but sees in a lot of other ways. His story is found in *Hope Unseen.*

ACKNOWLEDGE OUR SINFULNESS

Bartimaeus, in begging Jesus' help, also shows us how to utter a beautiful prayer. Notice how he didn't start off with himself but says: "Jesus, son of David, have pity on me." He was not like the publican in the temple who with his false ego thanked God that he wasn't like the rest of people. We can sometimes do the same: thank God I am not like people on welfare, homeless people, people who frequent x-rated movies--and the list can go on. We have to admit our sinfulness and ask Jesus to have pity on us also. St. Francis of Assisi considered himself the greatest sinner. Yet here was a man who carbon-copied the life of Jesus as perfectly as possible. He was known as the Christ of Umbria. The more we admit our sinfulness, our inability to see, the more we open ourselves to the healing power of Jesus. Hans Urs von Balthasar maintains that "sin obscures sight." It also leads to mediocrity which many of us enjoy, according to St. Teresa of Avila. Or the ego encourages us to brag about how good we are--like the bumper sticker, "I am damn good." Donald Trump refers to himself as "big, huge," which means not only his wealth and properties but his ego.

The story of Adam and Eve is a progressive alienation from

God, from one another, as well as from all creation. We often don't see how sin is an experience of alienation, isolation, and estrangement. Because of a false ego our response so often is, "That's not a sin anymore." If we have not lost our sense of sin, we certainly don't want to name our sin, and maybe, that is our greatest sin. Dante characterized hell not as fire but as ice because it shows how sin freezes us in the grasp of the ego. The proud person possesses a black hole which draws all its energy around the ego. The effects of pride are cleansed by a humbling of the ego.

Once Bartimaeus is cured, he immediately and eagerly follows Jesus. We too hear his call to follow the Lord but often respond, "Wait, I am not ready yet, or I have this or that to take care of in my life." We keep putting off what we know ought to be done in our lives. It is like going on a diet. Did you ever hear someone say, "I am going on a diet today?" We often procrastinate and wait until some other time. It is like the man who quit smoking, the day he died. We don't see how following Jesus is the only way because of his assurance that he is "the way and the truth and the life"(Jn 14:6).

Too often we take our faith for granted much as we take the air we breathe or our heartbeat for granted. David Steindl Rast admits that it "never ceases to amaze me that my body both produces and destroys 15 million red blood cells every second. Fifteen million! That's nearly twice the census figure for New York City. I am told that the blood vessels in my body, if lined up end to end, would reach around the world. Yet my heart needs only one minute to pump my blood through this filigree network and back again."[4] We leave our faith unattended as Bishop Kenneth Untener maintained, and as a result it does not grow and wax stronger but becomes flabby like unexercised muscles. Stephen Carter, a Yale professor, has written a book entitled *Culture of Disbelief*, where he points out that many people believe and teach that faith doesn't matter, rather that science and reason are more important. We are bound to be influenced by this type of culture. It is taught in many of our colleges and universities. So we have to ask ourselves: Is our faith a Current Affair or ancient history?

Many people see how important their faith is and get excited about it, especially those involved in the RCIA programs, Cursillo, Charismatic, Marriage Encounter, Teen Tech programs, or small group faith sharing communities. We have to learn how to savor our precious gift of faith much as a wine connoisseur tastes wine. I remember meeting a family in Detroit who were very excited about their faith and were willing to discuss their beliefs with each other in an animated conversation after a meal. They saw its importance in their lives and were trying to live that reality. Some novelists also get excited about writing another novel. The advice a famous novelist gave to his students was to notice what they see, and then trust in the significance of their observations. Too often we look at life with glazed eyes rather than zooming in on details.

We flinch and avoid what needs to be seen. David Liepert in *Muslim, Christian and Jew* hopes that Muslims, Christians and Jews can walk with their eyes wide open wherever they are.

THE COMPASSION OF JESUS

We need to see the way Jesus saw. He had compassion on the five hundred people in the desert who were there without enough food. He saw how they were like sheep without a shepherd. So Jesus took the five loaves and the few fish and was able to feed all of them with twelve baskets of fragments left over. Concerning this event, there is another interpretation which I like. One scripture scholar says that a number of people had more than enough food, so what they did was share with those who didn't. This is the challenge Jesus gives us: to see those who are in need and respond rather than throw up our hands in despair and say, "There is little that can be done" which the false ego encourages us to do. With God all things are possible. Do we really believe that? Is that how we live? One of our sins is our refusal to share with others. We want to accumulate more and more material things, thinking that will give us happiness and security. I don't come across too many people who say, "I want less." Pope Benedict XVI maintains that materialism gives us a sense of self sufficiency which becomes an obstacle to our life of charity. John of the Cross writes that materialism and secularism are illusions or subterfuges created by the ego which can never satisfy us. Only the infinite can. Materialism is a form of greed. Greed prompts the ego to desire and possess more than we need, refusing to respect other's rights, dignity and needs. Greed can often grow into a rage, which leads to violence against people and property. We often don't see that or are unwilling to admit this. Gandhi once said that there definitely is enough for everyone's need, but certainly not enough for everyone's greed. Greed is definitely a function of our ego. These people never live in the present moment because they want more and are never satisfied until they get it. They identify more with the future for its fulfillment. Nick Jagger's song, "I Can't Get No Satisfaction," is the mistaken voice of the ego.

The Apostles didn't believe it was possible to feed all those people. And yet Jesus did. The ego tells us that it is not possible to alleviate all the hunger in the world or even here in the United States. We might say, "How do you expect me to feed a hundred people or more?" Then we have to remember what Mother Teresa of Calcutta says, "Just feed one." If everyone did that much, we would help solve the hunger crisis. Pope Benedict XVI has encouraged us not to remain isolated and indifferent to others. We cannot mask our disinterest behind a sense of privacy.

Jesus saw Martha and Mary's pain because of the death of their brother Lazarus. He did something that showed his deep emotion, he cried. And the people responded, "See how much he loved him!"(Jn 11:36) When a loved one dies, we should not be afraid to express our feelings. I'll never forget when my father died. He died of cancer. Before he died, I remember standing next to his bedside and not being able to say much to him. I looked at him and he looked at me, and we didn't say a single word, but we spoke volumes in that exchange. When he died, I resolved that I was going to be the strong one in the family and not cry. At the funeral home I saw my mother crying, my two sisters crying, my younger brother and some of the relatives, and said, "Oh, well, why not join them?" That was the best therapy for me. St. Paul speaks of the gift of tears, and what a gift that can be for us and others.

Jesus saw the anguish of the widow who just lost her most precious gift, her only son. He came across this funeral at Naim and responded by raising her son back to life. I often say, "If only it were that easy when we lose a loved one--the ability to raise that person back to life or let go of the individual." But in so many instances this becomes most difficult and challenging, especially if the death is sudden or unexpected. If it is gradual, we still might question why did it happen? Our problem so often is that the ego tries to figure out why certain events happen and expend a lot of psychic energy searching for an answer. Life is a mystery to be lived not solved. We need to live what we don't understand as best we can. There is nothing wrong in asking why something happens, as long as we can live without the answer. We have to help others who are in mourning or in sorrow and act as a means of support to them in their grief. But very often we don't know what to say. We feel so powerless. It is not important what we say, because people will easily forget the words we utter. But they will never forget that we were there in their moment of grief.

BLURRED VISION

Too often we go through life with blurred vision or numerous floaters which prevent us from noticing something. Even dislike can darken our lenses. We really don't see. G.K. Chesterton wrote that when we stare at the familiar until it becomes unfamiliar, we will see it for the first time. The more attentive we are to each other, the more we will reach out to each other. Even if we don't know someone, we might be able to see his or her soul, despite the person trying to hide it. What a privilege it is for me to enter the library of another's soul in spiritual direction. The ego prevents us from taking the time to smell the flowers, to appreciate all the beauty around us, because we are in such a hurry or don't have the time. We more readily recognize beauty of the body rather than beauty of the soul. The ego entices us to look good. Just reflect on how forty-nine billion is spent on cosmetics or skin products, when much of that could be given to the poor and the hungry. No wonder we are blind to so many realities. Jesus pointed that out by saying, "seeing they do not perceive"(Lk. 8:10). "If one blind man leads another, both will end in a pit"(Mt. 15:14). You don't ask a blind person to lead someone else around. Jesus referred to the Scribes and Pharisees as blind fools. They thought they could help others because of their false egos, but really they should have been aware of their own blindness. They could not see that true love is much greater than any law.

This was their blind spot. And all of us have a blind spot, but we sometimes find it hard to see or admit what it is, just like the Scribes and Pharisees who could not admit their blindness. A good example of encountering a blind spot occurs as you are traveling on the freeway and you want to pass a car ahead of you. So you look in your rear view mirror and your side view mirror; all looks clear to pass. Suddenly, as you are about to pull out, you hear a horn blare at you indicating that there was someone right along side of you, but you didn't see the car. That is the blind spot. I have done this a number of times. As we go through life, we have to find that blind spot or area, or allow someone else to make us aware of it. Our blind spot might be jealousy or envy, being overcritical or judgmental of others, racism, sexism, some addiction, like alcohol, overeating, smoking too much, lust, pride or laziness. Ronald Rolheiser believes that we should not let the mosquito bites of life blind us to the much larger presence of grace. Many people are told that they need help, but they don't see the reason for it or will deny it. The ego can prevent us from seeking help when it is needed. The hardest words to say for some is "I need help." Often a spouse needs counseling but will refuse. The ego can be the worst enemy in marriage. I know of a couple where the wife refuses to get help, and now they are in the process of a divorce. Or a person who drinks too much will deny that he or she is an alcoholic. They don't see the damage they are doing to themselves or their children. They are in need of the healing power of Jesus to touch their lives, to remove the blind spots.

A certain marriage counselor always asks spouses who are ready to get married if they have any addiction in their lives. If they admit they have, she simply says: "You are already married, and this marriage will not work." Often these couples don't see or comprehend what this marriage counselor is trying to get across to them, because their false egos blind them or they say they are too much in love.

As people grow older and their eyesight begins to dim, they often need a cataract operation. What a difference that can make for them. Before the operation, their eyesight was blurred. After it, they can see much better. That is what happens to us when the healing power of Jesus touches us. Saul was blinded on his way to Damascus. Once the scales fell from his eyes, he saw what the Lord had in mind for him.

The great persecutor inverted his life and became the greatest convert worker the church has ever known.

Anne Dillard was born blind, but a brilliant surgeon was able to help her to see again. When the bandages were removed from her eyes, she immediately closed them. Everything, she admitted, was too marvelous, too beautiful to behold. She cried out, "Oh, God how beautiful, how beautiful." Maybe through the absence of our gifts we truly appreciate their value. God exclaimed every time something was created, "It is good!" We are the ones who spoil it. Pope Benedict XVI maintains that seeing beauty is a way to "ascend to God."

There is a story about two horses who look much alike until you get close to them. One of them is blind, but the owner has decided not to put him down. He prefers to make a good home for him, so he has attached a bell to the halter of the horse who can see. This enables the blind horse to know where the other horse is. If you watch closely, the horse with the bell is always checking where the other one is. When they return to the barn at night, the belled horse stops to make sure the blind horse is following him. At times we might be the blind horse and need to be guided out of our lethargy by a ringing bell. Or we might be the one helping or guiding someone else.

People with blurred vision, sometimes caused by false egos, have a tendency to blame others for their misfortune. Some even blame God because of what happens in their lives or the lives of their loved ones. Adam blamed Eve, and Eve blamed the serpent. So the cycle continues in our lives as well. We can blame a spouse, our parents, brothers, sisters, our boss, a neighbor, pastor, bishop or anyone else. In final analysis, we have to take the responsibility ourselves for the way we live our lives and stop blaming others.

Jesus did not blame others: to the woman caught in adultery, he simply said, "Go sin no more." He called Judas a friend even though he betrayed him for thirty pieces of silver. And to Peter who denied him three times, he didn't say a single word, but gave him a loving glance. That glance melted Peter's heart and converted him. Jesus always kept things in proper focus, and that is what we are challenged to do. A mistake we make is to focus too much on other's faults which the ego does resulting in a blurred picture. It is comparable to a camera that is not properly focused. What the camera produces is a blurred picture. Many people go through life with a blurred or jaundiced outlook on life and especially toward others. We need a wide angle lens to take in a broader picture of life. What a difference a wide angle lens makes. What a difference if we really see the true meaning of life and our relationships with others. To change the image, many of us are like horses with blinders attached. That gives them a narrow vision but prevents them from getting frightened by anything on their sides. Many of us don't want to see what needs to be done, because that might demand changing our lives or getting involved.

Mechthild Magdeburg, a thirteenth century mystic, considered the day of her spiritual awakening when she saw all things in God and God in all things. Thomas Merton wrote about how he was blind in his early life until he found himself in Corpus Christi Church in New York. He told his girl friend that he would not meet her as usual because a voice was telling him, "Go to Mass," which changed his life because of what he saw and experienced. Everything he saw after that was transformed, even sitting in a dirty restaurant at 111th Street in New York. He felt like he was sitting in the Elysian Fields as he records in *Seven Story Mountain*. To really see takes time, just like fostering a friendship takes time. No baby in the womb has a road map saying, "See, this is the way out!" If only we could understand and see how short our lives are and how our future lives will be eternal. It is difficult to store this in the attic of our minds or have it tattooed there, so we need to hit our reset button.

Most African societies greet each other with, "I see you."

We need to find ways to see people who are invisible like today's voiceless, weak, destitute, powerless, undocumented immigrants, not looking upon them as objects but as people loved by God. Many of us have seen slums and were repulsed by them. Maybe the best way to improve a slum or a ghetto is to put it out of existence, not just to displace it. All of us are called upon to help such projects. We need clarity to see through problems. Mother Teresa exhorted us to act as a light in the slums and lift the inhabitants up with a smile. We need to learn not to ostracize people or treat them as outsiders as our ego prompts us to do. Some day in judgment we are going to find the outsiders as insiders, and then all of us will be one.

A black clinical psychologist, Earl Brace of Glendale, Wisconsin, related how he was returning to his car after attending a Black Catholic liturgy. He encountered a white adult crowd. Looking into their eyes, he saw hatred, disdain and anger. He was hurt because he realized that the eyes are the windows to our souls, and Brace did not like what he saw. He believes with St. Augustine that we become what we receive. Brace emphasized the importance of parents teaching their children to respect others and themselves. Youth often don't want adults to tell them anything. Parenting skills are needed. Teenagers appear angry, but that does not excuse them lashing out at others. Community action is needed rather the efforts of city, county or state. Denominational forces need to band together to change the abnormal behavior or the erroneous path many of our youth are on.

Our vision has been blurred by not seeing the economic morass our country is in causing much suffering in the lives of countless people. Our economy has left millions mired in misery. Good jobs in the future will continue to be scarcer. Numerous economists have told us that this recession cannot be compared to any other. If workers were laid off in the past, there was always the hope that eventually they would be recalled. That is not true today because layoffs or pink slips have a finality about them. Many careers have ended after thirty years of faithful service and often without any benefits. We need to look for honest solutions such as scaling our standard of living and creating new jobs. We did not foresee the uprisings in Tunisia, Libya, Yemen, Egypt and Syria, and yet they happened. They were self propelled by the people. If it does not start with them, we have to see they really don't want us around.

GREATEST THREAT?

Many of us often don't see how the greatest threat to family life is the lack of time spent together. A need exists to spend at least one meal together. Some families take the time to meet together and discuss family concerns. Taking the children on a field trip once in awhile or some other activity fosters family ties. Setting aside time to do what the children like to do can tax parent's patience, but the results are rewarding. It certainly does not mean becoming a doting, hovering-helicopter parent which the ego wants.

We need to open our eyes to all realities around us the way Jesus did. He helped many people to see not only physically, but the broader perspective like Nicodemus whose vision was rather limited. There is a story about Gorbachev visiting the United States. He came across a boy who was guarding some small puppies recently born. Gorbachev asked him, "What kind of puppies are those?" The little boy responded, "They are Russian puppies."A few days later former President Bush and Gorbachev went by the same place and this time President Bush asked the boy, "What kind of puppies are those?" And the boy responded, "American puppies." Immediately Gorbachev said, "But I thought you told me they are Russian puppies." "Oh," the boy replied, "now they have their eyes open."

Now we have our eyes open. If only that could happen to us the way it happened to the disciples on the way to Emmaus.

They put all their faith in Jesus and saw him die on the cross. Their eyes convinced them that this was the end. Discouraged and downcast they left Jerusalem on their way to Emmaus. We know the rest of the story. Or do we? Because that is our story also-- how Jesus appeared to them and they didn't recognize him in his risen body. We need to recognize him in others as we recognize him in the breaking of the bread during Mass. Richard Rohr relates about his trip to Cape Town where Desmond Tutu told him, "We are only the light bulbs, Richard, and our job is just to remained screwed in."[5]

Once we are connected with Jesus, we will recognize him in the poor, the hungry, the lonely and reach out to them in a loving way. The final line in *Les Miserables* states that the person we love is the face of God. The Bishops, in their letter on the Economy, have challenged us to make a preferential option for the poor. That means the poor will be a priority in our lives which the ego tries to prevent. The poor can teach us so much about what it means to be a Christian and Catholic. The poor are like a mirror held up to us, reflecting our inner poverty. They cry out to us like a siren in the night, but our egos coax us to go right by them, not helping them in any way that we can.

The same is true of the hungry and the lonely. Capuchins run a soup kitchen at St. Benedict's in Milwaukee and also at St. Bonaventure's in Detroit. If we want to get a better picture of what hunger means, volunteer to help out at one of those places, or even better, stand in line to get a feeling of what these people must experience. In visiting home bound people in the parish, I often come across people who say how lonely they are. I remember in one parish where a laywoman accompanied me and her response was, "My, I never realized how lonely these people are and often frightened of the future." I know of a man who visits a nursing home every day after he finishes work which is certainly commendable.

When King Lear erroneously judged his daughter Cornelia

as disloyal and ordered her "out of (his) sight," Kent advised him, "See better, Lear."Jesus tells us how we are going to be judged some day. We are not going to be judged by how many Masses we have attended, how many Communions we have received, how many rosaries we have prayed. Not that these aren't important. They certainly are because they strengthen our faith and hopefully make it more dynamic. We are going to be judged by what Jesus said: "I was hungry, and you gave me no food. I was thirsty and you gave no drink, a stranger and gave me no welcome; naked and you gave no clothing, ill and in prison, and you did not care for me." Our response will be: "When were you hungry, when were you thirsty, or a stranger or naked, ill and in prison?" Jesus will reply,"What you did not do for one of these least ones, you did not do for me"(Mt 25: 42-45). Treating people as white, black, Latino, Muslim, homeless, mentally ill, addicted, ex-offender, gay, lesbian, often hinders us from seeing people as unique and real. Stereotyping, which the ego does, blocks us from acknowledging their rights, needs, dignity and potential.

Mother Teresa has said, "Our work calls us to see Jesus in everyone." If only we could do that, then we would see with the eyes of Jesus. Our eyes would truly be open because the healing power of Jesus has then touched us the way Bartimaeus was touched. So when Jesus says to us: "What do you want?" We, too, respond with Bartimaeus, "Lord, that I may see--with your eyes!"

SCRIPTURAL PASSAGES FOR REFLECTION

"Master, I want to see"(Mk 10:57).

"The lamp of the body is the eye. If the eye is sound, your whole body will be filled with light; but if your eye is bad, your whole body will be in darkness" (Mt 6:22-23).
"Blessed are the clean of heart, for they will see God" (Mt 5:8).
"Seeing they do not perceive" (Lk 8:10).
"The light shines in the darkness, and the darkness has not overcome it" (Jn 1:5).

QUESTIONS TO CONSIDER

1.What discourages you when facing some obstacles in your life?
2. Why do you miss or do not see the meaning of many of your experiences?
3. Do you see the need to embrace the cross in difficult times?
4. How can you see how materialism, consumerism are forms of greed and counteract them?
5.What is your blind spot and what are you doing to correct it?
6. Do you see how you might have a tendency to blame others?

CHAPTER TWO
CAN YOU HEAR ME?

"Daddy, when you listen to me, listen with your eyes,"said a five year old girl to her father who was reading a newspaper. Scott Peck, in his book *The Road Less Traveled*, maintains that a parent's willingness to listen is the best evidence of one's esteem for your child. We have been asked to remove the bandages from our eyes so we can see. Now we need to remove the earmuffs from our heads so we can listen.

Sacred Scripture brings out the importance of listening and acting on what we hear. Adam and Eve were told by God not to eat of the forbidden fruit. They certainly listened to God, but they also listened to the serpent who tricked them into believing that they would be like God, which is still the basic sin and the perfect illustration of the ego at work. This is how they edged God out of their lives. The Israelites were told that they were God's people and God would be their God. All they had to do was observe the commandments which they often failed to do. Moses had to intervene with God on their behalf many times. Abraham bargained with God about not destroying Sodom and Gomorrah if just a few good people were found. This highlighted how God was willing to listen to Abraham(Gen 18:16-33). God spoke to Jonah and told him to go to Nineveh, but Jonah didn't want to go because he was afraid the people would not listen or turn a deaf ear to his message of repentance. Job listened to all kinds of individuals like Eliphaz, Bildad and Zophar who gave him the wrong kind of advice, much like Bernard Murdoch did, so that people lost millions of dollars. In disgust, Job's wife said to him, "Curse God and die." Job replied, "We accept good things from God; and should we not accept evil?"(Job 2:9-10) He did not curse God as the ego probably encouraged him to do but blessed God. What Job had to learn was to listen to God and come to a realization of who God is.

We sometimes listen to the wrong advice which often the ego supplies, especially in this age of consumerism. We are bombarded each day by television, radio, newspapers, magazines to "buy, buy, buy, and, of course, pay later." We have to distinguish between our wants and our real needs. Often there are many things we want as the ego prompts, but we have to question ourselves, do we really need them? We are challenged to live a simpler life style, one in conformity with the Gospel. Jesus inspired us to travel light as we make our journey through this life. To the extent we are doing this, we are really listening to the right people and our true selves enabling us to live according to our Christian values of simplicity and identifying with the poor.

Samuel was called in the middle of the night and he immediately went to Eli because he thought that Eli was calling him. When Eli informed Samuel he was not calling him, Eli understood after the third time that it was the Lord who was calling him. Eli also told Samuel to respond, "Speak, Lord, for your servant is listening"(I Sam. 3:9). Samuel finally listened to what the Lord had to say to him. Our ego does not recognize when God speaks to us or refuses to listen because we would rather speak. Too often our ego helps us to reverse the process. When God speaks to us, we respond, "Listen, Lord, your servant is speaking," and edge God out. We have to learn to really listen the way Samuel finally did and allow God to speak to us.

At times, we also need to listen more closely, almost like fine tuning a radio. The radio station might not be coming in very clearly, or the sounds can be distorted or the sibilant sounds are very noticeable. Just a little turning of the dial can correct the matter. The same is true in listening to God and others. We have to fine tune our ability to listen. At other times, as Richard Rohr maintains, "If this inner and critical voice has kept you safe for many years as your inner voice of authority, you may end up not being able to hear the real voice of God."[6]

GOD SPEAKS TO US

Elijah was told by the Lord "Go outside and stand on the mountain before the Lord; the Lord will be passing by"(I Kgs.19:11). There was a strong and heavy wind, but the Lord was not in the wind; then an earthquake, but the Lord was not in the earthquake; after the earthquake there was fire, but the Lord was not in the fire. Finally, there was a gentle whisper. "When he heard this, Elijah hid his face in his cloak and went and stood at the entrance of the cave. A voice said to him, why are you here?"(l9:13) God was in that gentle whisper.

So often we expect God to speak to us in a certain way, or we already know what the answer should be. We have to learn that God can speak to us in a variety of ways, and sometimes in very gentle ways, at other times more forcefully. A most important aspect of listening is being open to whatever way God wants to speak to us because the ego closes many avenues. A whisper is a powerful way to get someone else's attention. A husband once told me that if he wanted his wife to listen to him, he would whisper to another woman. It takes more effort to whisper to someone. The same is true about the effort involved in really listening to God or others. Richard Rohr writes about "a deeper voice of God which you must learn to hear and obey in the second half of life. It will sound an awful lot like the voices of risk, of trust, of surrender, of soul, of 'common sense,' of destiny, of love, of an intimate stranger, of your deepest self, of soulful 'Beatrice.'The true faith journey only begins at this point."[7] The ego tries to silence these voices.

By listening to our inner voice, the true self, we might be able to hear God's voice speak to us. Pope Benedict XVI maintains that silence is of the utmost importance if we are to listen to

God. We are bombarded by the media and modern means of communication, resulting in a cacophony of information. Listening to God might seem like being camped out in right field. We need to listen even before the question can be framed. The answer often lies in darkness. Darkness comes unannounced and uninvited, but without it we cannot become the person we are meant to be. Do we dodge the mystery and the opportunity to be touched deeply by God's grace? Do we accept the raw edge of grief? Are we willing to accept God's blazing unpredictability? We inch our steps forward, hoping that they will lead to a much deeper union with God. St. Paul tells us that "faith comes from what is heard"(Rom 10:17).

God can speak to us in our suffering. It can become the tie rod connecting us to God. When we suffer, the ego is usually the cause because it provides all kinds of reasons why we are suffering. For the Buddhists, suffering is an illusion brought about by our clinging to egotism.

Richard Rohr in *Falling Upward* states "We, like the ox and St. Paul, largely still kick against the goad, instead of listening to and learning from the goads of everyday life."[8] He believes that the goads are necessary and even though suffering doesn't solve our problems, it reveals and opens up new ways for learning and living. Ken Keyes, a person-growth author, maintains that more suffering enters into our world by our taking offense than by our intending to give offense. When we are offended, we have a tendency to lash out at those whom we believe have offended us.

People in pain or trouble need a listening ear, but they also have to remember not to inflict more pain and suffering on others. A real challenge is listening to the ramblings of a mentally ill person, or the erroneous thoughts of an alcoholic or drug addict, which often masks their true identity. These are people who are broken, hurt and need to be comforted, sometimes carefronted, but always listened to patiently all of which the ego will refuse.

We don't realize how suffering and failure are cobbled together and can be equalizers in our lives. Success can often end in us having a superior attitude and everything is rosy and upbeat, the result of the ego. We fail to hear the cry of the poor for support and understanding when we are too concerned about our need to succeed. The ego is caught up in the success game of competition. When we experience failure, the true self needs to ask "What can I learn from this? Or, "How is God present is this tragedy?" When suffering is accepted, God's love can shine through us as it did so forcefully in the saints. Even though suffering causes us many tears, it can express our vulnerability and fragility which the ego often tries to hide from others.

When the Dalai Lama visited the United States, he was asked why the Buddhists have a marvelous attitude to overcoming suffering. Christians, on the other hand, often wallow in their suffering. He responded, "It is not as easy as all that. Suffering is not overcome by leaving pain behind; suffering is overcome by bearing pain for others."[9]

JESUS LISTENED

If anyone really listened it was Jesus. This is evident throughout his life. At his baptism and the transfiguration, the heavens are opened and the Father says, "You are my beloved Son; with you I am well pleased"(Lk.3:22); and at the transfiguration, "This is my chosen Son; listen to him" (9:35). Probably one of the reasons why the Father was so pleased with his son was that he really listened. His whole life might be summed up, as some spiritual writers suggest, when he said to Mary and Joseph, after being found in the temple, "Did you not know that I must be in my Father's house?"(Lk. 2:49) He always wanted to do what the Father asked of him. And to do that, he listened and obeyed. Obedience comes from the Latin word *ob-audire*, which means to listen or hear. We often forget that Jesus, who was God, was obedient to Mary and Joseph. Jesus did not find it easy to listen to what the Father asked of him. That is evident in the Garden when he was asked to die for us. He prayed, "Father, if you are willing, take this cup away from me; still, not my will but yours be done"(Lk. 22:42). Thomas Merton believed that we possess a false self, one that exists outside of God's will and love. Sin enters when everything centers around one's egocentric desires. Once we find God, we find our true selves. It is very difficult for us to understand what the Father was asking Jesus to do for us besides dying. It was to take on our sins or become sin for us. That explains why St. Luke, a physician, could write, "his sweat became like drops of blood falling to the ground"(22:44).

Our response might be, "oh, that's impossible." A Doctor Barbet has written a book entitled *Doctor at Calvary.* In this book he shows how it is possible that a person can suffer so intensely that the capillaries of one's body actually break and the blood oozes out. That probably happened to Jesus. But Jesus was willing to listen to what the Father asked of him and comply with that wish despite how wrenching it was. Fortunately, we are not asked to go to that extent, but we certainly are encouraged to listen the way Jesus did to so many people he came in contact with. He listened to the woman at the well; Nicodemus who came to him at night; Jairus, who wanted his daughter cured; Bartimaeus who wanted to see, just to mention a few.

WE OFTEN DON'T LISTEN

We spend 40-60% of our day in listening, but how much do we really listen or hear and thereby edge God out? Many of us have what is known as selective hearing. We hear what we want to hear, but what we should hear we make believe that we don't hear it. Others have a hard time hearing, because over 28 million people are hard of hearing in the United States. A recent study shows that hearing declines twice as fast in men as in women.

When Joseph's brothers came to him for grain in Egypt, they did not recognize him, but he, knowing them, locked them up for three days. Then Joseph instructed them to bring back their youngest brother while another of the brothers had to remain in prison. The brothers realized that they were being punished. Ruben even says, "Didn't I tell you, not to do wrong to the boy? But you wouldn't listen!"(Gen. 42:22). Vatican spokesperson, Father Frederico Lombardi, insists that the Church needs to listen to victims of abuse as a permanent and integrated part of its life.

To prove that people don't listen, a newly wed man, while standing in a reception line, said to the people as he shook their hands, "My grandmother died last night." Few, if any, heard what he said. His bride did hear him and kicked him in the shins. Now whenever either one is not listening to the other, he or she says, "My grandmother died last night." President Theodore Roosevelt was known as a good listener and did something similar. He was so bored at a gala event because of the mindless pleasantries, Roosevelt greeted people by stating "I murdered my grandmother this morning." Because most people were so nervous in meeting him, they did not hear what he said, except one diplomat who responded, "I'm sure she had that coming to her."

Some people refuse to get hearing aids not because of the cost involved, but the inconvenience of wearing them. They would rather not hear or listen but keep on asking the question "What did you say?" when others speak to them. I am amazed how many people adjust their hearing aids when a person begins a lecture or is listening to a homily. I don't want to be judgmental, but I wonder if they are turning their hearing aids up or off at homily time. At times we have to tell others something over and over again because they did not hear us the first time or were not really paying attention. One man complained that no one really listened to him, so he asked that the following words be inscribed on his tombstone, "I told you I was sick."

At times we do find it hard to listen because of all the noise around us. Boom boxes and radios are blaring, sirens are screaming and our egos love it. One of our friars loved to play his music really loud. So one of the friars asked him, "Do you like it loud?" He responded, "What did you say?" Experts point out how hearing loss has increased among people in their 30's and 40's due to noise. How do we find meaning in the noise of the news? Recently, Pope Benedict XVI encouraged young people to sift through "the many voices of the world" so they can hear Christ's voice.

We come in contact with what we call trouble makers. Often they are not bad people. They have a tendency to move down Trouble Lane. Just as we possess a right and left brain, we have two interior ears. One of them longs for true relationships and service to others. The other ear, belonging to the ego, longs for self indulgence, mischief and self destruction. Which ear do we attune to Jesus' message, challenging teachings of loving our enemies or those who persecute us or get on our nerves?

Representative Walter B. Jones of North Carolina, admitted that he voted for the war in Iraq because he did not listen to his conscience. He did not listen to what God was telling him, but now he is a staunch opponent of the war in Afghanistan. Jones believes we need to speak out when the government cuts programs for children and senior citizens, as well as realizing how corrupt the government is in Afghanistan. He maintains that if we are not listening or watching what is going on in Afghanistan, we will suffer even more tragedies by edging God out.

ACTIVELY LISTENING

We have to learn to actively listen the way Jesus did to so many with whom he came in contact. To actively listen means to listen with a third ear, or with our heart. That is what Jesus did, and it explains the tremendous compassion he had for people. I often ask small children, "Why did God give us two ears and only one mouth?" You certainly hear some humorous responses to that question, like "we would look funny with two mouths." But the real reason is that we can listen more than we talk, and so often our tendency is just the opposite. Some people just have to learn to talk less and listen more which contradicts their egos. They often shoot from the lip too fast, and in many instances regret what they have said. One of the reasons for so much talking is the emphasis placed on self expression. Mark Twain is supposed to have said that it is better to be thought a fool and keep your mouth shut, than to open it and remove all doubt. Another piece of good advice is to speak only when you'll be able to improve on the silence.

Lydia, a dealer in purple cloth, listened to Paul when he came to Philippi. As recorded in the Acts, "The Lord opened her heart to pay attention to what Paul was saying." She and her whole household were baptized, and then she invited Paul to her home. As Paul said, "she prevailed on us"(16-14-15). Nothing like a little arm twisting or persuasion.

People often don't really hear what we say to them. A wife asked her husband, "Will you love me when I am old and grey?" He said, "I do!" Or a man might not know what a woman is trying to convey. Mildred said to Bob, "Do you realize that we have been seeing each other for five months?" Silence ensues. Mildred does not know how to interpret that, whether he is upset or thinking that it is a long time. But Bob might be thinking about something else--the long time since he has spoken to his aunt. Unless Bob breaks the silence, Mildred won't know what he is thinking, so she has to remind Bob over and over again about their relationship and what that means to her. Listening was important in this story of a priest who one day received an urgent call to come to a home. When he arrived, he found the husband holding a gun on his wife and children. The priest calmly said, "Tell me your story." After ten hours of listening, the man gave him his gun. If we are going to listen actively, something within us has to die which the ego resists. To actively listen to someone else means we give our undivided attention to the person and something within us has to die. Jesus said, "Unless the grain of wheat falls in the ground and dies, it remains just a grain of wheat"(Jn 12:34). Active listening means we hear not just with our head but with our heart, which enables us to listen not only to what the person says, but also to what the person does not say. Some times what the person does not say is more important than what the person says. It also means that we have to empty ourselves of our distractions, of what we are going to say next, of the tendency to cut people off before they finish what they are saying, or complete their sentences. If we are conversing or trying to listen to boring people, that becomes an even greater challenge. Some people have a tendency to repeat themselves or are incoherent in expressing their thoughts. This kind of dying or emptying is very difficult at times, but a powerful way to counteract the ego and help us become active listeners. We need to listen to the young, helping them discover their own path in a struggling society. They can be encouraged to use their energy in building a more peaceful world.

PEOPLE WHO ACTIVELY LISTEN

Mary listened to the angel Gabriel when he announced to her she was to be the mother of God. Her ego wanted nothing for itself as she proclaims, "My soul proclaims the greatness of the Lord," but only being a vessel giving honor to God (Lk 1:46). Oprah Winfrey is not only a good communicator but also a better listener. She constantly listens to find issues relevant in our society. This is evident by her listening to celebrities and what they have to say. Her previous show attracted over thirty-three million people. Oprah initially had doubts about one of the ideas presented to her--a book club. But by listening and taking the risk, this idea had phenomenal success. She listened to others to make her present show, OWN, even more fun.

Ada Maria Isasi-Diaz, a leading voice of mujerista (liberation) theology, spent three years in Peru, listening and trying to understand the practices of the grassroots people. She spent weekends listening to women telling her who God is in their lives. She considers this the kernel of mujerista theology. When women tell her their stories, she feels like she is a monstrance carrying the stories.[10]

Dorothy Day, as recorded in *The Duty of Delight: The Diaries of Dorothy Day,* used to enjoy listening to Brahm's First Symphony. She did this, despite being bothered by Margaret who wanted some butter, Tom asking for pencils, and the baby fretting. But she was convinced what we listen to one day might not give us the same enjoyment the next. James Garner tells the story of how he learned the importance of listening in the Broadway Production *The Caine Mutiny Court Martial.* He played the part of one of the judges in a military court. For two hours on stage he did not say a single line, but he learned that the most important part of acting was listening.

The ego deadens the cry of the poor for support and understanding because we are too concerned about our own needs and success. Serving the poor might sound romantic until we find out how lazy, manipulative and addictive some can be. They can even steal your shoes or harm you, resulting in distancing yourself from them. A real challenge is actively listening to the ramblings of a mentally ill person or the erroneous thoughts of an alcoholic or drug addict. These are people who are broken, hurt and need to be comforted and listened to, but also need carefrontation at times. People in pain or trouble need a listening ear, but they also have to remember not to inflict more pain and suffering on others.

Archbishop Gregory Aymond of New Orleans was willing

to listen to the people of Our Lady of Good Counsel in the city. They were very upset when their church was closed in 2008. Archbishop Aymond listened to their pain, disappointment, anger and was willing to bring about reconciliation. The church has now been taken over by a charismatic Catholic community and is called Center of Jesus the Lord, but it will not be a parish or offer parish programs. It will be used for Mass and other charitable activities. Former parishioners can use the building for weddings and funerals. Listening fosters mutual understanding and counteracts the obstacles we experience at times.

OBSTACLES TO LISTENING

John Maxwell in *The Indispensable Qualities of a Leader* states, "I would say that the overwhelming majority of communication problems come from poor listening."[11] The problems we have in listening to others can also center around being judgmental which the ego urges us to do. We often have to ask ourselves how much we value other people's opinions. It was evident from the life of Jesus that he valued other people's opinions and was not judgmental. He did not judge the woman caught in adultery but told her to go sin no more. He didn't return the rudeness on the part of the Samaritan woman when she said to him, "How can you, a Jew, ask me, a Samaritan woman, for a drink?"(Jn.4:9) We often judge others by their appearance, the type of car they drive, the home they live in, the clothes they wear. We sometimes say, "so and so is a good Christian, so and so, not so good." We probably will be in for a few surprises when we get to heaven. People we expected to be there aren't there; others we never expected to be there will be there. And maybe the greatest surprise is that we are there. I have learned the hard way not to judge others. I remember being in a first grade classroom and saw twins sitting up front of the other children. I said to them, "You two must be twins."

Another child in the back of the class popped up and said, "No, we are triplets." I had put two and two together and got twenty-two. This next incident actually happened in a parish. Some people were coming up to receive Holy Communion wearing motorcycle helmets. Sure enough, someone went up to them saying"You can't receive Holy Communion wearing motorcycle helmets." So they walked out of church. Later on this individual found out that they were told to wear them by their doctor because they were subject to epileptic seizures. Jesus said, " Stop judging, that you may not be judged"(Mt 7:1).

A tendency also exists on the part of the ego to want us to be in control of others, and so we really don't listen to them when they speak to us. This is very evident in family situations. A power struggle is sometimes evident between spouses or parents and children. They really are not listening to each other because they want to control the other or the situation. So often teenagers will complain that their parents "just don't listen to them." But how much do they listen to their parents? One of the basic problems in family life is that individuals really are not listening to each other. Kids will often not listen when lectured by their parents. Lectures are some times a way to control the children, especially when they are not given an opportunity to speak.

Jesus was the master listener and can teach us how to listen. We need to slow down our lives. In the hustle and bustle of our activities in our topsy-turvy society we just don't have time to listen to others. Our lives can be compared to a freeway existence, where it is rush, rush, rush. Did you ever notice how few people really observe the speed limit? We are constantly in a hurry, rushing here and there which the ego enjoys. What we have to learn to do is slow down and pull over on the roadside of life, especially into a spiritual oasis and take the time to really listen to God, to others and ourselves. Jesus said to his Apostles: "Come away by yourselves to a deserted place and rest a while"(Mk. 6:31). St. Mark tells us, "People were coming and going in great numbers, and they had no opportunity even to eat. So they went off in the boat by themselves to a deserted place"(6: 32). Doesn't that sound familiar? We have to find that place also where we can really listen and be open to how God speaks to us.

God can speak to us in silence which the ego abhors. But many of us are uncomfortable with silence. Or people will often say, "I listen to God, but God doesn't say anything." Then we have not listened, because God can speak to us by not saying anything. He has spoken to us through his Son, Jesus, and everything else is an echo. Silence of the heart, as experts point out, makes listening possible. We have to learn to silence ourselves before we can actively listen. Silence is not a blank, but the pregnant possibility of what is about to be born.

An uncomfortable kind of silence exists when another person refuses to speak to us. That can be a clever way to get even with us which is certainly encouraged by our ego. Jesus experienced this when he cured the man with the withered hand. He asked the Pharisees, "Is it permitted to do good on the Sabbath rather do evil, to save life rather than destroy it?"(Mk. 3:4) St. Mark tells us how they remained silent, and how Jesus became angry because they had closed their minds. People can close their minds like rusty bear traps when they do not like what is said. The book of Ecclesiastes tells us that there is a time to keep silence and a time to speak (3:7). Jesus had that amazing ability of when to speak and when not speak. If it is true that God's first language is silence and everything else is a translation, we can learn to actively listen to what God has to say to us in silence. The psalmist puts it well, "Be still and confess that I am God"(46:11). God tries to tell us to stay in the tomb, but we want to come out after the first day at the urging of the ego.

We also have to learn to actively listen to others, to what

the Church says, Pope Benedict XVI, or those in authority say. Some people will retort, "I don't care what the Pope says, what the Bishops are saying, or what my pastor says." It is sad when some people close their minds the way the Pharisees did, and not at least be open enough to listen what the Pope, Bishops and pastors are saying. Friends can some times tell us things about ourselves or our behavior that we don't like to hear. Leonardo DiCaprio lamented the fact that one of the pitfalls to his success as an actor was he did not listen to criticism. He believes that we have to hear criticism of ourselves and embrace it. How open are we to accept criticism and act on it? A friend can often challenge us, but we have to listen and act on what the individual tells us. A doctor can often tell us something we don't want to hear: go on a diet, quit smoking, or need an operation. Too often the ego prompts us not to take the advice, or convinces us that we are the writers, directors and stars of our own movies.

We also need to listen more actively to our own bodies. Our bodies are marvelous in letting us know what is going on within us. But so often the ego tells not to listen. We know we should see a doctor, a dentist, a psychologist, but we keep putting it off or refuse to do so. Too many people have paid the price of procrastination or the refusal to really listen to what their bodies are trying to tell them. Our bodies do not lie.

Listening more attentively to our feelings will tell us so much about ourselves. We are not responsible for what we feel, but we are responsible for what we do. The feelings of anger, impatience, jealousy, as well as many others need to be faced and embraced in our lives not ignored or repressed as the ego prompts us. The sooner we do this, the more healing can take place and we will more readily reach out to others. Our task is to help remove the toxins of weariness, using the antidote of a big smile and a listening ear. In this way we find relief from the poisons of complacency and aggravation.

While in China, Father Matteo Ricci S.J., was insightful

enough to present the Gospel in a meaningful and new way to the Buddhists. They actively listened to him and he was well accepted. As his influence grew, however, the other orders became jealous of his success and reported him to Rome which resulted in the suppression of the mission. It reminds us of Jesus' words "The kingdom of heaven is like the head of the household who brings from his storehouse both the new and the old" (Mt 13:52). How open are we to the new as well as the old?

We are a busy people with many distractions like cell phones, computers, ipods, television, texting, just to mention a few. Even when we might be listening, our brains are constantly chattering. We might not have enough time to tell someone, "That's interesting, tell me more." Experts point out that we retain only one-quarter of what we hear. When we are not listening we are not learning. How many courses are there in schools devoted to listening? Living life to the fullest requires active listening. So maybe like the deaf mute, we also need a lot of healing in the area of actively listening to God, others and ourselves. Jesus says to us, the way he said to the deaf mute, "Ephphatha! that is, be opened" (Mk 7:34). And to the extent that we actively listen to God, others and ourselves, the healing power of Jesus can touch us deeply as well and can bring healing to others.

SCRIPTURAL PASSAGES FOR REFLECTION

"Go outside and stand on the mountain before the Lord; the Lord will be passing by" (I Kgs 19:11).
"A time to be silent and a time to speak" (Eccl 3:7).
"This is my chosen Son; listen to him" (Lk 9:35).
"Come away by yourselves to a deserted place and rest a while" (Mk 6:31).
"Ephphatha! that is, be opened" (Mk 7:34).
"Faith comes from what is heard" (Rom 10:17).

QUESTIONS TO CONSIDER

1. How does God speak to you in your daily life, in your suffering?
2. Why do you find it hard to actively listen to others?
3. Why do you prefer to talk rather than listen?
4. What do you think is your biggest obstacle to actively listen?
5. How can you listen more to your own body or your feelings?

CHAPTER THREE
TENDER, LOVING TOUCH

Some time ago I came across an article entitled "Have you Touched Anyone Lately?" The subtitle was "Try it; it can work wonders." The author points out how there is a deep-seated hunger within everyone of us that no amount of food can satisfy. The hunger is to be touched or what some refer to as "skin hunger." We live in a society, however, where we have to be so careful in touching another for fear of sexual harassment. The ego is certainly operative when considering the sexual abuse of children. Appropriate touch can heal, soothe, but used improperly can destroy.

One of the most serious problems the Catholic church faces today is the sexual abuse of children by the clergy. It is difficult for us to grasp how these offenders did not know how their behavior violated and harmed innocent children. According to the John Jay Report, there was a failure on the part of diocesan leaders to take full responsibility for the harm done. Why Bishops and other church officials allowed known offenders to be shuffled from parish to parish is mind boggling. Some bishops addressed the problem, but others, called "laggards," did not. Now we are feeling the impact of those decisions.

What is the largest organ in our body? It is our skin. It guards our muscles, bones, ligaments and other organs. Some years ago Brenda Peterson wrote *Nature and Other Mothers,* where she narrates how she was suffering from painful skin rashes. She tried contacting various doctors like the woman with the hemorrhage in the Gospel but was unsuccessful. Doctors would suggest a remedy, but the rashes would return. Her grandmother finally came up with a remedy.

She gave her skin massages. Sure enough, the rashes disappeared. Brenda was cured and entitled her first chapter

In Praise of Skin.
Of the five senses, touch is the only one that doesn't decrease as we age. We have seen how our eye sight as well as our hearing decreases with age. Animals need to be petted. Penguins need to be touched to survive. House cats rub themselves around objects, and dogs love to have their ears and stomachs stroked. Most people hug one another when meeting. We touch others when crammed into a subway, train or crowded room. But some try to avoid those encounters as much as possible. Many men have difficulty hugging their counterparts. We e-mail, text, twitter, Facebook, blog, skype or use other means of communication, but often feel uncomfortable or even loathe physical closeness. Experts tell us that people who have loved ones to touch on a regular basis actually live longer and happier lives. They also maintain that a light, appropriate touch of the arm can influence the way we think, and we might even give a waitress a bigger tip! Don't we use the expression like "I was touched by your kindness?" Or "Stay in touch," or "lose touch?" We also use the expressions, "heavy handed," or "thick skinned." Babies need to touched, cuddled, loved and held so their true self can grow and develop normally. Babies deprived of skin contact can lose weight, become ill and even die. And who doesn't love a good massage! Massage therapists will attest how touch can heal and soothe, but when used improperly can be damaging.

A pat on the back, a high five, a hug doesn't seem like much, but they communicate a powerful message. Some psychologists who have analyzed professional basketball teams have determined 15 kinds of touch, high fives, shoulder bumps and hugs. Their conclusion is that the teams who touch the most win the most. Dacher Keltner, a psychologist professor from the University of California, maintains that touch is our primary language of compassion. The emotional and physical health benefits can never be underestimated.

Loving and tender touch can be transcendental reaching the highest levels of closeness, our intimacy with God and others. Our egos resist closeness or intimacy. Our problem is that too often we associate touch exclusively with sexuality. In the Book of Daniel we read, "The one who looked like a man touched me again and strengthened me"(10:18). Dr. Virginia Satir of Wisconsin recommends that we need four hugs a day to survive, eight for maintenance and twelve for growth. Seniors are the least touched in our society maybe because our culture associates youthful skin as more touchable. Another reason might be because many live alone.

It is very evident from the Gospels how often Jesus touched others and was touched by them. Jesus was accused of being a wine bibber, a cohort of the devil, a blasphemer, but no one leveled any sexual impropriety or abuse against him. Jews would have been considered virtually unclean if they touched a dead body. Jesus willingly touched the daughter of Jairus to restore her to life. Recall also how a leper approached Jesus and asked to be cured of his leprosy. Jesus was not afraid to touch him, even though he risked ritual impurity because of the Jewish law. Touching a leper made a person legally unclean. Lepers were considered cursed by God. When they approached a town or city, they often had to ring a bell or cry out, "unclean, unclean," and people would scatter. The ego tries to prevent us from coming near them. The famous historian, Josephus, wrote that lepers were considered dead people. No other disease was considered so hideous.

A number of years ago I had the opportunity of visiting the only leprosarium here in the states. It is located in Carville, Louisiana. I remember most vividly seeing some lepers, and the story of Father Damian immediately flashed through my mind. These lepers were brought to the island of Molokai by boat and often the lepers were thrown overboard before they got there. Those who could swim made it, the others drowned. Father Damian being true to his true self spent sixteen years of his life on the island and eventually contracted the disease. One Sunday he started his homily in the most powerful way, addressing them: "My fellow lepers." I also found out while visiting in Carville, that these lepers make various articles which are sold in the neighboring stores. It would be interesting to find out how many people would buy them, if they knew where they came from. Would you?

Francis of Assisi had a great revulsion for lepers in his early years because his ego kept him aloof. In fact, when he traveled through an area where the lepers lived, he would hold his nose. But one day he got off his horse and kissed a leper. That became a turning point in his life.

He suddenly became aware that this person represented Jesus crying out for help. We need to ask what or who is the leper in our lives? Some people have a leper list of people whom they dislike, even hate or have nothing to do with them. We need to counteract our ego and embrace the leper in our lives whoever or whatever that is.

Jesus was asked by Peter to cure his mother-in-law. We often forget that Jesus had just finished preaching in the synagogue and he was probably tired. I know how tired I can become after preaching a parish mission. When I return to my community in Milwaukee, often someone will say,"Richard, could you help me do this?" My ego often urges me, "Let me alone, I need time for myself and I am tired." This happened recently and I did the task. Jesus could have reacted in a similar fashion, but he took Peter's mother-in-law by the hand and the fever left her. On another occasion, children were being brought to Jesus and he laid his hands on them in prayer. The disciples began to scold the mothers, but Jesus said, "Let the children come to me, and do not prevent them; for the kingdom of God belongs to such as these"(Mt. 19:14).

We might ask ourselves how do we feel when certain words are brought up in conversation: "unwed mothers," "people with disabilities," "welfare people," "mentally ill," "cancer victims," homosexual," "people with AIDS?" Our ego would exhort us to stay away from them. On parish renewals I have visited many home bound people who have cancer. They told me that they used to have a lot of friends, but now many of them will not come to see them because they are afraid of contracting cancer. The same is true of people who have HIV or AIDS. Nothing is further from the truth. How many of us are willing to reach out and help them? When homeless, jobless, displaced persons, immigrants appear at our doorsteps, do we act like Dives ignoring Lazarus? We need to remember where our grandparents came from. Sister Joan Chittister keeps a rock from her grandparent's house in Ireland as a reminder that she is tied to her Irish heritage.

JESUS TOUCHED MANY

Jesus touched many people. He put his fingers in a deaf man's ears and touched his tongue (Mk 7:33). He touched the ear of the man whose ear Peter severed and healed it (Lk 22:51) He healed the boy possessed by a demon and "took him by the hand, raised him, and he stood up"(Mk 9:27). Jairus made a decision to ask Jesus to come and "lay your hands" on his daughter because she was seriously ill (Mk 5:23). Jesus learned before he departed that the girl had died. When he came to the place he said, "Why this commotion and weeping? The child is not dead but asleep" (Mk 5:39). They began to ridicule Jesus. If we have ever been ridiculed or laughed at, we know what Jesus must have felt like on this occasion. Our ego will make every effort to avoid any kind of ridicule or being made fun of by others, but encourage us to return the coin of unkindness. We need, however, to rise above this and be determined to live our Christian principles, values and ideals. It is not easy and most challenging in our secularistic society. People will some times say, "Ah, come on, you don't believe that, do you?" or "Get with it, everybody is doing it."

I know of a very close friend who is considered weird because she will not involve herself in the common gossip around the shop, or the water cooler interplay. Some revel in talking about the foibles of others. She often challenges or carefronts them, reminding herself what would Jesus do? But people like that often feel so much alone, or the ego will have them wonder if there really is something wrong with them.

Jesus took the girl's hand and told her to get up. Jews would have considered themselves unclean if they touched a dead body. She immediately stood up and began to walk around. What is very touching is how Jesus told the family to give her something to eat. It is easy to overlook the obvious at times, but Jesus was very conscious of that and reminds us also to be more conscious of other's human needs, especially their need to be touched in a loving, caring way. Experts insist that some children deliberately misbehave so they are spanked. In this painful way their skin hunger is somewhat satisfied. Fortunately, there are homes where children have their skin hunger satisfied by the hugs or compliments they receive. These children tend to be more open, warm and relaxed. Ever hear of a bumper sticker asking and reminding parents, "Did you hug your kid today?" In contrast, the false ego strives for attention by the way we dress, the way we behave, the way we talk. These people have no center so they are shattered when experiencing some traumatic or tragic event like a divorce or the loss of a loved one.

Jesus' touch was not a pat on the back but rather a loving communication. When he appeared to the Apostles at the transfiguration, it symbolized inner healing and a deeper awareness of who Jesus was. It was an interior embrace, dispelling fears and anxieties. Jesus also touches us when we are overwhelmed by doubt and uncertainty. Did you ever notice that once Jesus touches the Apostles they "no longer saw anyone but Jesus alone with them?"(Mk 9:8) This demonstrates the power of interior touch, enabling us to see

Jesus in all events and circumstances. It helps us to live from our inner being, our true self, so we can reach out to others who are in much greater need than ourselves.

KEEP YOUR EYES FIXED ON JESUS

Jesus was aware of the need Peter had to be helped when he walked on the water and started to sink. The main problem with Peter was that he took his eyes off Jesus. As the book of Hebrews tells us, "persevere in running the race that lies before us while keeping our eyes fixed on Jesus, the leader and perfecter of faith"(12:1-2). When Peter became startled thinking of what he was doing, he suddenly became more aware of himself, the false self or ego, rather than focusing on Jesus. And later in Hebrews we read, "Make straight paths for your feet, that what is lame may not be dislocated but healed"(12:13).

Life can deal us some hard blows at times which become real tests of our faith. I met a family where their 24 year old son contracted cancer, and then the father lost his job. These events and similar ones can test our faith. We feel like Peter and can easily sink into depression or become discouraged. But Jesus is there to help us, provided we keep our eyes fixed on him. I will never forget the man I visited in a hospital. The first thing he did was to tell me, "Father, I almost did it." And my question was, "Did what?" "I almost committed suicide," he replied. Then he went on to tell me his story, how he was divorced, lost his job, and none of children had anything to do with him. We all have a story, but the problem is that we don't have enough listeners. At that point he reached for a small crucifix which he showed me. "Do you see what happened to this crucifix?" I noticed that the corpus on it was broken. He told me that he squeezed the crucifix so hard when he was ready to take his life that the corpus broke. "But," he went on to say, "that saved my life." Every time we look at the cross and fix our eyes on Jesus, we are reminded that he saved our lives. "For the sake of the joy that lay before him he endured the cross, despising its shame"(Heb. 12:2).

St. James tells us, "Consider it all joy, when you encounter various trials, for you know that the testing of your faith produces perseverance. And let perseverance be perfect, so that you may be perfect and complete, lacking in nothing"(1:2-4). People who are able to patiently endure their trials and see them in relationship to Jesus become better and not bitter individuals. Their true self enables them to be patient. In times of difficulty, discouragement, depression, or the death of a loved one, a hug is most appropriate. "Reach out and touch someone," was a famous commercial made by AT&T. But do it in a loving, tender way.

Jesus gave us a powerful demonstration of his love and caring by washing the feet of his Apostles on the night before he was to die. This was an act reserved for a slave and it was Peter's false ego who protested that he would never allow Jesus to do that to him. Jesus said to Peter, "Unless I wash you, you will have no inheritance with me"(Jn. 13:8). Peter was then ready to have not only his feet washed but his whole body. I sometimes have what I call a towel and water service where individuals are invited to pour water over the hands of another and then dry them. Reluctance is often shown on the part of some not to have their hands dried by the other person. It demonstrates how we can easily resist having things done for us. We can become independent and won't let people minister to us. This becomes evident to me when people suffer a stroke, and they are no longer capable to do things for themselves. Many find this a very searing cross in their lives. But they often have not prepared themselves for such an eventuality. We are more willing to minister to others rather than have others minister to us. The reason might be because we are not in control. It is easier for some to love than to be loved.

The touch of Jesus was also meant to arouse spiritual senses. John rested on the bosom of Jesus at the Last Supper, close to his heart where he was immersed in divine love. John felt interiorly embraced by Jesus. Did that enable him to follow Jesus to the foot of the cross, whereas the others abandoned him?

JESUS TOUCHED BY OTHERS

Jesus allowed individuals to minister to him or to touch him. We read in Luke's Gospel "Everyone in the crowd sought to touch him because power came forth from him and healed them all"(6:19). Recall the woman with a hemorrhage of twelve years and how she tried numerous doctors before going to Jesus. What we often forget about her is that she was considered unclean because of her illness, so she could not worship with the community. She was an outcast for that length of time. The Talmud gave no fewer than eleven cures for such an illness. One of them was carrying the ashes of an ostrich egg in a linen rag. She undoubtedly tried various tonics, but none of them worked. Still she was embarrassed to tell Jesus aloud, so she touched his clothing and was cured because of her deep faith.

Here was a woman who did not give up even after ten or eleven years. Imagine the adversity she encountered during that time. Our adversity can be looked upon as obstacles or opportunities. The ego looks upon them as obstacles, but the courageous person views them as opportunities. A person's true character is revealed the way one deals with adversity. How easy it is to give up. Read a story of a twenty-year-old man who while driving a truck veered off the road and plunged into a thirty foot dried up riverbed. He was hospitalized and in a coma for nineteen years. His mother visited and spoke to him encouraging him as only a mother can during all those years. One day while attending to him, she asked him "Who is here?" He woke up and said, "Mom."[12] She never gave up just as the woman with the hemorrhage who undoubtedly was surprised when Jesus said, "Who touched me?" She was hoping to sneak away without being noticed.

St. Luke tells us about a " sinful woman in the city" who learned that Jesus was dining at Simon the Pharisee's house. As someone so aptly put it, she crashed the party, bringing with her some perfumed oil. She "stood behind him at his feet weeping and began to bathe his feet with her tears. Then she wiped them with her hair, kissed them, and anointed them with the ointment" (7:37-38). Because the jar of ointment was broken, the aroma filled the whole house. Jesus' body was broken on the cross and the "aroma" filled the whole world. Simon and his guests were horrified. This story demonstrates how two people can love each other chastely. It is hard to imagine that the physical contact was not sensual. But was there anything sexually inappropriate? Evidently not. Simon's ego prompted him to object that Jesus would allow a sinner to touch him. He had closed his mind like a rusty bear trap to the possibility that Jesus had come to bring back those who had strayed away.

In the process Simon forgot the common courtesies shown a guest. Jesus told Simon "her many sins have been forgiven; hence, she has shown great love"(7:47). She demonstrated her love. That is the only kind of love which is credible. Shakespeare maintains that they don't know how to love who do not show their love in his *Two Gentlemen from Verona.* We are challenged to show our love especially with those with whom we live and work with each day. It is so easy to withdraw from others, especially when we are hurt by their remarks. They can burn our ears. Some feel good by putting others down, or it makes them feel better by making others feel bad. So the businessman criticizes his secretary for her computer mistakes, or the telephone message she forgot to relay. A mother can be over critical of her daughter because of her unkempt room.

A driver might say, "Look at that idiot who is trying to drive." The impression these individuals give us is, "I am better than they are," another example of the ego taking over. The richest sea in the world is the Dead Sea. Yet nothing can live in the sea despite the fact that all the tributaries flow into it. Why? Because there is nothing flowing out. Jesus showed and demonstrated his love for us most powerfully by his death on the cross where he shed his last drop of blood for us. He said, "No one has greater love than this, to lay down one's life for one's friends"(Jn. 15:13). That is the ultimate of one's love for others, and Jesus touched all our lives by this heroic act.

In the passion we recall how Judas and the soldiers "stepping forward they laid hands on Jesus and arrested him"(Mt 26:50). From then on all kinds of cruelty was done to Jesus showing us his meekness and humility. Once Jesus rose from the dead he encountered Mary Magdalene by the tomb. She did not recognize him and thought he was the gardener. But once he said her name, "Mary," she knew who he was. She evidently wanted to cling to him so Jesus said, "Stop holding on to me; for I have not yet ascended to the Father"(Jn 20: 17). At times we want to cling to others or find it so difficult to let go of a loved one. Widows and widowers often struggle when their loved one dies. But they have to remember to look beyond this life where they will be reunited with their spouse far more intimately than here on this earth. Recently I told this to a woman who lost her husband, and she exclaimed, "Oh, no!"

Parents usually find it hard to let go of their children once they have grown up and especially if they have strayed away from the faith, joined a cult, gone through a divorce, or declared them-selves homosexual. The hurt can often be very great. But parents have to continue to be patient, love and pray for them. The mother of Augustine went to St. Ambrose one day and told him about her son's wicked life. He told her to continue to love and pray for him which she did for twenty years, and he finally converted. She became something she didn't even pray for: a saint. We honor her as Saint Monica. I'll never forget the man who said to me, "What do you mean I have to love my daughter when she is shacked up with this man and they aren't even married?" My response was, "You don't have to condone what she is doing and let her know that, but it is most important that you continue to love her." St. Paul says it well, "Love never fails"(I Cor. 13:8). The highest kind of love which Jesus showed during his lifetime touched the lives of many people, especially sinners.

It is this love that has to motivate us also to reach out and touch others who are in much greater need than ourselves. Suzanne Rose started a volunteer organization called Pilgrims of Hope. She ministered in a Jamaican nursing home for the elderly who had been abandoned by their adult children. She would often uncap a small bottle of lotion, put it into her hand, and then rub it into the dried crevices of their bodies. They responded to her touch by caressing her arm. She believes that of all the loneliness experienced by people, the denial of human touch appears to be the most inhumane. Her touch has softened their hearts and helped them to speak out about their families and their memories which they often refused doing.

An Irish Dominican, Paul Murray, tells the story of how he was one day in deep conversation with Mother Teresa who certainly lived Jesus' message of reaching out to the least of our brothers and sisters. When Paul ended his talk, she asked him to extend his hand while she touched each of his fingers individually and said to him, "You did it to me."

EARLY CHURCH
The power of touch was carried out in the early church as is evident from the Acts of the Apostles. Peter and John went up to the temple to pray and they came in contact with a cripple who begged for an alms. Peter said to the cripple,

"Look at us!" The cripple expecting to get something, looked at Peter and John. Peter said, "I have neither silver or gold, but what I do have I give you; in the name of Jesus Christ the Nazorean, (rise and) walk!"(Acts 3:4-6) Peter took the cripple by the hand and pulled him up and he began to walk. What I like about this story is they gave what they had. We often hear people say, "I don't have much to give to the church or some charitable organization." Then they have to give what they can. And if we don't have the money, then their time and talent are always appreciated. Recently at a parish in Brooklyn, New York I met a lady who is a librarian for the school and she is over a hundred years young. Time is one of our most precious commodities. But we have to learn to give of our time to others the way Jesus did. He did not have office hours and was always available to respond to the needs of others. We can also touch the lives of others through our prayers.

We read in chapter nine of the Acts how Ananias laid hands on Saul and scales fell from his eyes as he recovered his sight. The early Christians would fast and pray, then impose hands on their missioners and send them out (Acts 13:3). Paul told the presbyters at Miletus, "You yourselves know that these hands of mine have served my needs and my companions"(Acts 20:34). We also read in the Acts that even handkerchiefs and aprons that touched by Paul were taken to the sick and the believers were cured.

Do we ever stop and reflect on how much we have accomplished with our two hands? They can be used for good or evil. The physical abuse they can cause staggers the mind. Many horror stories of child and spouse abuse have been told. What we need are more caring and loving people who are willing to touch us gently and lovingly. Daniel Berrigan once declared, "It all comes down to this: Whose flesh are you touching and why? Whose flesh are you recoiling from and why? Whose flesh are you burning and why?"[13] We come into the world needing to be touched and that need continues until our dying breath. No way exists to measure the amount of healing that has been done through tender, loving touch. We are touched through the various sacraments of baptism, confirmation, Eucharist, and the reconciliation, especially when we receive it face to face. It is impossible to determine how much healing has been brought to us through these sacraments. We have so much to be grateful for, especially the use of our hands. Have we ever taken the time to thank God for all that we have done with our hands?

Some days we can feel like we would rather stay in bed than be involved in grunt work barely making a salary. The ego often invites us to stay there. David Patrick Columbia experienced this until he started on his way to work counting the things that made him happy. He noticed a mother taking her child out in a stroller, a plane in the sky, the smells of the various bistros he passed. By the time he arrived at work he was thankful for so many good things that he had taken for granted. His gratitude-strolls enabled him to keep him focused.

Science has proven that being grateful can be beneficial to our health. By being grateful which the ego tries to prevent, we acknowledge the blessings in our lives. Some people when asked how they are, respond, "I am blessed." Gratefulness will enable us to sleep better, feel more alert and active. In an experiment conducted by two psychologists, Robert Emmons and David Patrick, they asked one group of people to concentrate on what went wrong in their lives. The other group had to concentrate on what enhanced their lives and made them grateful. The second recorded fewer headaches, colds and other negative physical symptoms. They also noticed how joyful, energetic, optimistic they were and their ability to reach out and touch someone. Gratitude can makes us more compassionate, social-minded and less materialistic. They also found the second group less envious, anxious and not prone to depression.

Loving, tender touch and being touched can make each of us much better people. Jesus continues to give us the example in his life. He shows us how to establish better human relationships, how to treat each other with more love and care, how he touched and was touched by many people. Jesus reminds us that loving and tender touching can be healing and soothing, that it can be the primary language of compassion, the compassion he used to cure and heal many people. Tender and loving touch is transcendental, reaching the highest levels of our closeness to God and others.

SCRIPTURAL PASSAGES FOR REFLECTION

"The one who looked like a man touched me again and strengthened me" (Dan 10:18).

"Jesus took him by the hand, raised him, and he stood up" (Mk 9:27).

"Unless I wash you, you will have no inheritance with me" (Jn 13:8).

"Everyone in the crowd sought to touch him because power came forth from him and healed them all" (Lk 6:19).

"Her many sins have been forgiven; hence, she has shown great love"(Lk 7:47).

QUESTIONS TO CONSIDER

1. Are there people you dislike or even repulse you? How do you respond to them?

2. How do you keep your eyes fixed on Jesus?

3. Do you resist having people ministering to you like Peter did?

4. Do you find it hard to reach out and touch someone in a loving, caring way?

5. Have you ever thanked God for the gift of your hands or any other gifts you possess?

CHAPTER FOUR
HIGHEST KIND OF LOVE

What will motivate us to see with the eyes of Jesus, actively listen to God and others and touch in a loving, tender way is showing the highest kind of love. Jesus challenged us to this kind of love when he said, "Love your enemies, do good to those who hate you, bless those who curse you, pray for those who mistreat you. To the person who strikes you on one cheek, offer the other one as well"(Lk 6: 27-29). Our ego will tell us that we are unable to accept that challenge? Robert P. George, a Catholic advisor to many presidents and U.S. Catholic bishops, maintains that love of enemies is likely the most radical of Christ's teachings because it is so contrary to reason and our natural emotions. One atheist who started reading Matthew's gospel came to this section on loving your enemies and stopped reading because he considered this "hippie nonsense." We have bumper stickers that say, "Show an Act of Kindness Today," but have you ever seen one that states, "Love those who hate you?" Pope Benedict XVI in his encyclical *God is Love* speaks of an *agape* love which is this higher kind of love, a love that consumes, a love that is self-sacrificing, a love that is unconditional, a love that transcends eros and phileo love. Eros love is based on strong, romantic love, whereas phileo love is based on friendship. Agape love does not wait to be acted upon. God's love for us is active, always present despite what mistakes we make. Agape love continues when all the others quit, cares when there isn't any reason to care. It is totally selfless and given without any benefit whether returned or not. Agape love has been described as the cross extending its arms to all the world. It appears at least three hundred and twenty times in the New Testament, three times in *Euripides* and ten times in Homer.

Love means willing the good of another as other. This

love would prevent wars, counteract all kinds of violence so prevalent in our society, racism, sexism and many other isms. It would establish a new order of peace, justice and mercy. It is the rarest kind of love demonstrated by the mother of the Maccabees along with her seven sons who were arrested, and forced by the king to eat pork which was a violation of the law. Six of the sons were killed in hideous ways before her. The mother encouraged them, saying that God "in his mercy, will give you back both breath and life." One son remained and the king urged the mother to save him, but overcoming her ego to save him, she encouraged him, saying, "Do not be afraid of this executioner, but be worthy of your brothers and accept death, so that in the time of mercy I may receive you again with them"(2 Mc 7ff). The mother also died after her sons.

We read in 2 Maccabees of Eleazar, a scribe of advanced age-ninety, who was forced to eat pork. Refusing the meat, he spat it out and was led to be tortured. Those in charge of the unlawful meal even took him aside and urged him to bring his own meat and pretend to eat it and thereby escape the death penalty. But he would not listen to his ego, and deciding not to do this said to them, "At our age it would be unbecoming to make such a pretense...I will prove myself worthy of my old age." He went immediately to his torture, stating he was willing to suffer "with joy in my soul because of my devotion to him"(6:18-31). Eleazar left a model of courage and of outstanding love not only for the young but also for the whole nation.

Judith provides a vivid story about how God used her love of the Jewish people to deliver them from death. Having fasted and prayed, she goes to the Assyrian camp which was ready to defeat and conquer the Jewish people. Judith, fortified by prayer, was successful in killing Holofernes the commander of the Assyrian army. The Assyrians panicked and the Jews were able to rout and defeat them. This event strengthened the faith of the Jewish people in God's abiding presence.

Maximilian Kolbe demonstrated the purest and holiest of loves, a total sacrificial kind of love. He provided shelter to Jewish refugees and was arrested in 1941 by the German Gestapo. Kolbe was imprisoned in Pawiak and later transferred to Auschwitz. Three prisoners disappeared from the camp and the deputy picked ten men to starve to death in a bunker to prevent further attempts at escape. When one of the men chosen cried out, "My wife, my children," Kolbe volunteered to take his place. Another man who showed much love and care was John Quinn, owner of a bar in Boston. He heard about Franklin Piedra, a 33 year-old Ecuadorian, suffering from chronic kidney failure who was in need of a $100,000 kidney transplant which he could not afford. Quinn had saved his money for a major down payment on a two bedroom apartment with a river view in Boston, but decided to forfeit all of his money for Franklin Piedra.

The highest kind of love does not ask favors or a reward in return. Do we love others for what they can do for us? We use the expression, "You owe me." Jesus said, "If you love those who love you, what recompense will you have? Do not tax collectors do the same?"(Mt 5:46) When we are good or kind to others because they are good or kind to us, that can be a form of egotism. As Robert Barron maintains, "When we love we escape the black hole of our own clinging egotism and live for someone else; to love is to leap ecstatically out of self."[14] The highest kind of love is willing to suffer persecution and persevere. Are we willing to accept suffering or pain, or do we try to shut it out of our lives by escaping from it? It is related in the life of Clement Hofbauer, a Redemptorist, that he collected money for his boys' orphanage. One day he approached a man and asked him for a donation. The man spat him in the face and said, "Take that, and go." Clement responded, "Now, that was for me, how about something for my boys?" The man was so disarmed by this, that he dug into his pocket and gave him all his money.

Abraham Lincoln stated that he destroyed his enemies by making them his friends. A seminarian asked his Bishop how it was possible to love your enemies and not hate them, especially when they continue to hurt you? The Bishop responded that you hate them a little less each day and thereby counteract your ego. With every person, whether difficult or loving, we need to remember that we are interacting with the divine which is most challenging.

The greatest love story ever told is not the movie or musical *Gone with the Wind* as advertized in 2007, but the story of Jesus's birth. Soren Kierkegaard called faith in the incarnation a commitment to the absurd. Our problem in appreciating this event is that we have heard the story too often and it has become threadbare like tires on a car. We need to be renewed by the heartbeat of a small child wrapped in swaddling clothes who some day would be wrapped in a linen cloth and laid in a tomb.

A story is told of World War II, where the Nazis rounded up Jesuits and sent them to concentration camps together with Jews, gypsies and homosexuals. One of the nuns had to endure the horrific experiments of a Doctor Josef Mengele who was known as the "Angel of Death." With his white coat and outstretched arms he determined who was sent to the gas chambers and who were sent into forced labor. Mengele used inmates to experiment on heredity and was very interested in identical twins and dwarfs. He drew a line on the wall at the children's block, and those whose heads did not reach the line were sent to the gas chambers. His assistant was a woman, a nurse, who administered these torments. While the nun was suffering, she took a rosary from around her neck and gave it to the nurse who immediately recoiled from the offer. The nurse asked what she was doing. The nun replied that it was a gift and asked her take it. Her last words were a blessing before she died. Undoubtedly, compassion and forgiveness had become part of this nun's life which enabled her to resist the temptation to strike back like the ego desires.

FORGIVENESS THE KEY

Forgiveness is the key that unlocks much of our resentment, anger, revenge and hostility which are encouraged by the ego. It frees us from toxic emotions which can shackle us. Some theologians speak of the parable of the lost sheep as the scandal of the particular. Even dislikes can darken our lenses. Some will say that they will forgive others provided the other party apologizes first. That statement indicates we do not understand the highest kind of love which always takes the initiative. God did not have to create this world but out of love God did and said, "It is good." Did you ever notice that Adam and Eve never said they were sorry for their sin, but God takes the initiative and promises a redeemer for us, Jesus, God's most precious gift to us? Jesus always took the initiative in reaching out to sinners and forgiving them and asks us to imitate him. The prodigal father takes the initiative and runs to greet his lost son.

Jerome Kodell, O.S.B., abbot at the abbey in Subiaco, Arkansas, tells the story of a man who was a voter register in the Mississippi delta. He was asked if this wasn't dangerous especially during 1960's when the racial struggle was white hot. He responded, "It's true the hatred is vicious, and the punishment is violent." "Have you ever been hurt yourself?" "Yes, I've been spit on, beaten with fists, with pipes, with chains and left a bloody mess." "But you're pretty big. Weren't you able to protect yourself sometimes, to fight back?" "Yes, at first I did fight back. I made some of them sorry they had attacked me. But then I realized that by fighting back I wasn't getting anywhere. The hatred coming at me in those fists and clubs was bouncing right off me back into the air, and it could just continue to spread like electricity. I decided I would not fight back. I would let my body absorb that hatred, so that some of it would die in my body and not bounce back into the world. I now see that my job in the midst of that evil is to make my body a grave for hate."[15]

When I read this story, all I could say was "Wow!" This man showed agape love. It is most challenging not to fight evil with evil which the ego invites us to do. St. Paul tells us "Do not be conquered by evil but conquer evil with good"(Rom 12:21). His insight is truly deep, profound and courageous. Jesus also did this in his experiencing an excruciating scourging, insults and an ignominious death which led to his resurrection. By accepting our suffering, insults, hardship, all of it is transformed by the power of the Holy Spirit into our resurrection. C.S. Lewis described agape love as the highest level of love known to us, a selfless love passionately committed to others. I Corinthians 13 conveys what agape love is: patient, kind, not jealous, not pompous, not inflated, not rude, not quick tempered, not brooding over injuries, and bearing all things. The opposite are weapons of the ego. Agape love forgives someone no matter what a person has done.

Even though we might find it difficult to forgive, or we some times hurt others, God continues to love us. God woos us into knowing how much we are loved. God does not want our consolation but our intimacy. We are certainly worth more than what we produce. St. John of the Cross maintained that God refuses to be known but wants to be loved. A rift exists at times between our inner experience and our outward behavior because of our ego. But no rift is possible with God's unconditional love because there are no strings attached. If we would ever grasp or feel deeply how much God loves us, we would blush. God's love does not coerce but coaxes.

A very capable minister at the University of Scranton, Pennslyvania, was leading a prayer service for some students. She asked them to imagine Jesus in front of them and to look him in the eye while they prayed. Later she asked one of the students how the prayer went. One of them hesitantly admitted that she could not do it because she was unworthy. Jesus loves us despite our unworthiness, because he loves all sinners. In *The Cloud of Unknowing* we read that it is not what you are presently, or what you have been in the past. What God sees is what you desire to become.

God's love shows itself in action not just words. Tony Blair tells the story how a teacher knelt with him as they prayed for his ill father. Tony said, "I'm afraid my father does not believe in God." The teacher replied that it did not matter because God loves him without demanding or needing love in return. That inspired Tony Blair to understand God's unconditional love and undoubtedly helped him convert to the Catholic faith. Only a person who is poor and humble can accept God's unconditional love. A sign of God's love, according to Quran, is unity. Unity has played a most important part in Islam which means oneness, not sameness.[16]

JESUS SHOWED HIS LOVE

Jesus showed us the highest kind of love by dying on the cross. He stated that "No one has greater love than this, to lay down one's life for one's friends"(Jn 15:13). He did it. Army Spc. Dennis P. Welchel Jr., while serving in Afghanistan, noticed children collecting shell casings at a range to sell for scrap metal. A ten-year old Afghan boy darted under a vehicle which was ready to move. Welchel immediately climbed under the vehicle and pushed him to safety while the huge vehicle ran over and killed the soldier.

Kahil Gibran in *Prophet* states that Jesus gave everything. Father Solanus Casey, a Capuchin of the St. Joseph Province located in Detroit, exclaimed, "I want to give until there is nothing left to give." Mother Teresa told her sisters to give and give until it hurts. She believed that the human heart functions best when at the service of others. We need to be reckless in our love which the ego abhors. Imagine what could happen. St. Bonaventure wrote that love does not consist in isolation, but rather in reaching out to others. He believed that the Trinity was an example of perfect love. To love God with our whole heart, mind and soul, means to love God with everything we possess. That becomes our challenge in our relationship with others. The ego will convince us that is impossible, but we believe that with God all things are possible.

Julian of Norwich, a 14th century mystic, believed it was in our Lord's passion where she learned the true meaning of love and love for others. Paul and Barnabas showed the highest kind of love as they hop-scotched their way through Lystra, Iconium, Antioch, Derbe and Pisidia. They were very successful but also encountered many difficulties as Jesus did. They had to suffer many hardships comparable to a mother's birth pangs which Jesus spoke about. But their suffering was accompanied by a joy and peace which the world cannot give. They always remembered that Jesus is the message, they were the messengers.

Richard Rohr writes that the litmus test for knowing if we are in the second half of our lives is, do we love what we have, or do we have what we love? Hoarding, collecting, wanting more, being greedy, are possible signs that love is being squeezed out of our lives. Another way of edging God out of our lives. Too often we love what we should hate, and hate what we should love. And that can apply to ourselves. When Jesus stated, "Love your neighbor as yourself," he did not say "Love your neighbor as much as yourself." What Jesus was getting across to us was that your neighbor is yourself. St. Bernard believed that the hardest kind of love is to love oneself. Freud could not believe this was possible. The ego believes it but in a narcissistic way. It means to recognize our worth and go deeper into the well of our goodness. Is this one reason why some Christians don't love others, because they don't love themselves?

Just outside of Memphis, Tennessee, members of the Heartsong church welcomed an Islamic faith community to use their church. They were moving and were not ready for Ramadan, so in an act of Christian hospitality Heartsong church invited their new Muslim neighbors to use their church building. They have shared meals together, worked together at a homeless shelter, and have bonded with each other. The minister, Steve Stone, was accused of being a heretic. Steve responded that he was doing what Jesus taught, "to love our neighbor." Lee Raines, a blues musician, was against the idea until he read the Good Samaritan story in Matthew's gospel. The offer took many of the Muslim members by surprise, and some felt uncomfortable using the building. Some members of Heartsong left their church, while others acted as greeters during Ramadan. Now plans are being made for a park which both could use. If we want to build bridges between Christians and Muslims, why not start with someone whom both faiths love and admire: Jesus? The highest kind of love continues to write a chapter of keeping faith, hope and love alive for a better future.[17]

You might have heard or read about two small boys born in Iraq with birth defects who were thrown away in a shoe box. Their limbs were also damaged by chemical warfare in Iraq. Somehow they were found, and an Australian woman, Moria Kelly, dedicated to disadvantaged children, brought them back to Australia. Seventeen years later, Emmanuel Kelly, the older brother, appeared before an audition on the X Factor to sing, "Imagine." He wowed the judges as well as the audience and has pursued a singing career. Other examples of agape or the highest kind of love are: donate to charities even though you never met any of the people who are the recipients; pushing a stranger out of the path of a moving vehicle while putting yourself at risk; putting someone else first even though they do not deserve it; always seeking the best for others.

LOVE CAN TRANSFORM OUR LIVES

The highest love transforms us into Christ's likeness and unites us more intimately with him. The ego uses all its powers to prevent this. Couples who have been married for fifty or more years and are still deeply in love have been transformed by each other. They are more attuned to one another. Mary Pipher in *The Shelter of Each Other,* writes about family ties, how Fred, her grandfather, would never go anywhere without telling his wife Agnes how much he loved her. He added how lucky he was as a man to have married her. The highest kind of love shares deeply with loved ones all the secrets of their hearts. This love becomes more transparent as was true in the life of Father Walter Ciszek S.J., whose transformation happened by enduring excruciating suffering while imprisoned in Siberia. He spent fifteen years in confinement and hard labor in Gulag and Moscow's infamous Lubyanka prison. The experience enabled him, however, to radiate Christ even more to others once he was freed. How we act under stress will determine what we become. All of us were created in a unique way to manifest God's love in the world. For women to convey this love was a source of contention in the Middle Ages because they were considered (and still are in some ways) inferior to men. God certainly did not create them that way.

For Francis of Assisi the transformation took place when he embraced a leper. Previous to this he despised them because of his ego. Once, however, he embraced and kissed the leper, what before seemed loathsome was changed into what he called sweetness. Now he was able to minister to them calling them his "Christian brothers." Those kind of experiences show us how religion does not become a matter of do's, don'ts and obligations but one of joy and consolation. It becomes relational not harsh and dogmatic.

Accepting suffering, according to Father Gerald O'Collins,

S.J., can be the highest form of transforming love. Bishop Walsh spent twelve years in a Chinese prison. When finally released, he was asked if this was the kind of reward he received for toiling with these people. He admitted that he held no animosity against the Chinese who imprisoned him. Nelson Mandela was imprisoned for seventeen years and emerged a changed man. St. Paul from his prison cell encouraged the Philippians, "Rejoice in the Lord always. I shall say it again: rejoice!"(4:4) The irony is that we grow by falling apart; some need to hit the bottom or experience the dark night of the soul before change takes place. But we often cry out, "Isn't there another way?" The lotus plant is embedded in a dark, muddy pond, but once it blooms, it is beautiful.

The highest kind of love is a love inflamed with fervor and poured out for the sake of another enabling us to become vital members of Christ's body. When the Saracens attacked the monastery of Clare of Assisi, she had the Blessed Sacrament brought to her. Clare then prostrated herself and declared herself a hostage so that her sisters would not be harmed. They were not and the Saracens left. Like Jesus she was willing to lay down her life as well as desiring to go to Morocco to endure martyrdom.

It is possible to willingly die for someone, but at the same time be seething with revenge and anger at the person. John Shea tells the story about a woman who invited her aging mother to live with her while she was recovering from a stroke. While being attentive to all her needs, fights ensued as trivial as over a hard boiled egg. One day the mother asked, "Why are doing all this for me anyway?" The daughter responded, "I was afraid of her; I wanted her well; I felt maybe I ignored her when I was young." She also gave many other reasons. The mother was so impressed that she told her that all those reasons were not necessary because they loved each other which was enough. When two people fall in love and their love is directed not only to each other but also to God, then their love will deepen and wax stronger. If their love is directed just to each other, it probably will result in shared egotism.

A higher kind of love often rests at a deeper level. Even when we say, "Good morning," to a person, a peck on the cheek, a brief hug, and find it hard to do it because we are not feeling well, that shows love and care for the person. Ritual acts like these and others sustain our faith and love. Dorothy Day stated that where there is no love, put love. She believed that no matter how damaged and battered we are by life's trials and difficulties, we are still bearers of God's image in the world. Resistance to the highest kind of love will continue to plague us causing us furrowed brows and pursed lips. So we need a bone deep commitment to show it not just a notional assent. Highest love can start a revolution. Jesus started this by declaring a revolt against unjust systems, the disenfranchised, the marginalized, the oppressed and the poor. In Shakespeare's *Midsummer Night's Dream* and *As You Like It,* several of the characters dismiss love as a "madness" leading us away from the real world. Love led John, Mary and the other women to the cross.

Too often we think of love as romantic rather than what Jesus had in mind. The ego might convince us that we are gracious and most loving. Jesus, however, continues to challenge us to love everyone as I have loved you, not when we feel like it or only certain people. Have we forgiven those who have hurt us or even ourselves, and maybe sweat blood as Jesus did in the garden? Have we taken the high road when ignored, rejected, misunderstood, or had recourse to bitterness and resentment? Someone at an AA meeting put this sign up on the bulletin board, "Resentment is a luxury we cannot afford." How willing are we to die for people who oppose us, continue to mistreat us or get on our nerves? Jacques Maritain's faith was tested when he saw his wife die. He wrote that there are two kinds of people who think love is easy: saints who made self sacrifice a habit in their lives, and naive people who have no idea what they are talking about.

Mother Teresa of Calcutta captured the imagination of the world and also her many followers when she stooped picking up a dying man. But we don't have to show this love by addressing the United Nations or attending a summit meeting. Divine love takes the first step as Mother Teresa did and we might also witness results beyond our vivid imaginations. If a single thought can change the universe which the mystics believed, then divine love can also have deep and profound effects which our ego is preventing from happening.

When Jesus was invited to Simon the Pharisee's house, he omitted the signs of welcome: water to wash the feet, head anointed with oil and a kiss. The woman, noticing this, provided the courtesies in a loving way by weeping many tears on Jesus' feet and wiping them with her hair. She poured oil over his feet and kissed them. This should have caused Simon to be ashamed, but as Thomas Keating points out in *Reawakenings,* his superego got in the way and he blurted out, "If this man were a prophet, he would know who and what sort of woman this is who is touching him, that she is a sinner"(Lk 7:39). Jesus reprimands Simon for his lack of courtesy and forgave the woman because she manifested great love. The formula for true and lasting transformation is demonstrating divine love. Once we see that all is a gracious gift of God, we will be willing to show the gift of highest love to all as saintly people did. That is our challenge.

St. Theresa at the age of ten was bedridden and intensely suffering not only physically but psychologically, often giving way to convulsions. She noticed a beautiful statue of our Blessed Mother which had been placed in her room. Mary was smiling. Suddenly, she was healed which cannot be explained except as God's love penetrating her whole being. Once she entered Carmel she had to learn to break through the needs of her ego by doing ordinary things such as putting up with an annoying sister, showing her excessive love. Theresa gradually found her vocation, love.

When we arrive at our destination of heaven, faith and hope will cease but love will endure as St. Paul assures us, because we will see God who is love. We will not be awarded a spiritual sky box, or maybe not Peter saying in a few stained glass words "Well done, good and faithful servant." Heaven will help us understand what the highest or fullest love is, especially that it will never end. All that is not love will be burned away.

SCRIPTURAL PASSAGES FOR REFLECTION

"Do not be afraid of this executioner" (2 Mc 7:29).

"No one has greater love than this, to lay down one's life for one's friends" (Jn 15:13).

"Love your enemies, do good to those who hate you, bless those who curse you, pray for those who mistreat you" (Lk 6:27-28).

"Do not be conquered by evil but conquer evil with good"(Rom 12:21).

"Love is patient, love is kind. It is not jealous, (love) is not pompous, it is not inflated, it is not rude..." I Cor 13: 4-5).

QUESTIONS TO CONSIDER

1. How can I show the highest kind of love?
2. Do you find it hard to forgive others or yourself?
3. How has love helped you to transform your life?
4. Are you willing to die for someone who opposes you?
5. Do you believe that by showing the highest kind of love it will lead you to the cross?

CHAPTER FIVE
MISUSED GIFT

One of the ways we don't show the highest kind of love or edge God out of our lives is misusing our gift of speech. Some years ago I visited a home bound man who had fourteen operations in twelve months. He contracted cancer of the tongue and was advised to have his tongue removed. So he could not speak, and we carried on our conversation by means of a pad of paper. Whenever I said something, he would write on his pad, and thus we carried on our conversation. I'll never forget something that he wrote: "Father, we'll do anything to keep alive."

That is so true because one of the strongest impulses we have is self preservation. Of course this does not always apply to people who are deeply depressed or want to commit suicide. But it is true for the majority of us. Undoubtedly, this man realized what a marvelous gift we have in our ability to speak and be healthy. Speech is a gift that we often take for granted much like we take the air we breathe for granted. It is also a gift often misused.

The Scriptures reveal to us how God speaks to us. After Cain kills Abel, God asks Cain where his brother is. Cain responds, "I do not know. Am I my brother's keeper?"(Gen. 4:9) He certainly knew where he was and what he had done. Later, in Chapter Eleven we read that the whole world spoke the same language, using the same words. But the people wanted to build a tower into the heavens so they might become more independent of God. The sacred author tells us, "Thus the Lord scattered them from there all over the earth, and they stopped building the city. That is why it was called Babel, because there the Lord confused the speech of all the world"(Gen. 11:8-9).

When God appeared to Moses in the burning bush, God

asked him to go to the Pharaoh and lead the Israelites out of Egypt. But Moses responded, "If you please, Lord, I have never been eloquent, neither in the past, nor recently, nor now that you have spoken to your servant; but I am slow of speech and tongue (Ex. 4: 10). So God suggested Aaron to Moses who accompanied him.

When God called Jeremiah to be a prophet to the nations, he replied, "Ah, Lord, God! I know not how to speak, I am too young."And the Lord said, "Say not, 'I am too young.' To whomever I send you, you shall go; whatever I command you, you shall speak"(Jer. 1:6-7). And what an impact Jeremiah had on the people he spoke to at his time. When called by God to serve as a prophet, Isaiah considered himself a man of unclean lips, living among people of unclean lips. Isaiah tells how "one of the seraphim flew to me, holding an ember which he had taken with tongs from the altar. He touched my mouth with it. 'See,' he said, 'now that this has touched your lips, your wickedness is removed, your sin purged'"(Is. 6:6-7). The book of Isaiah has continued to be a source of inspiration to countless people.

God can speak even through an ass, as is related in the story of Balaam and his ass. As the sacred author writes: "But now the Lord opened the mouth of the ass, and she asked Balaam, 'What have I done to you that you should beat me these three times?'"(Num. 22:28) Gradually Balaam understood that it was the Lord speaking to him and had to acknowledge his sin. This is a powerful example of how nothing is impossible with God. As one pastor claimed, if God can use an ass to speak, he can certainly use me.

Zechariah, Elizabeth's husband, did not believe the angel Gabriel when he told him that his wife would conceive and bear a son who was to be called John. Zechariah would not believe this because Elizabeth was far beyond child bearing age. So he was struck mute, unable to speak until he was asked the child's name. He wrote on a tablet that his name was John. John the Baptist was the golden link between the Hebrew Scriptures and the New Testament. He spoke a powerful message of repentance at the River Jordan and told the tax collectors, soldiers and people what they were to do. He stood up against Herod and told him he had done wrong by taking Herodias as his wife. As a result of his speaking out so forcefully, he was thrown into prison and had his head cut off. Jesus gave him one of the finest compliments when he said, "among those born of women there has been none greater than John the Baptist"(Mt. 11:11).

But all the prophets, including John, pale into insignificance with the coming of Jesus. The prophet Isaiah had said of him: "The Lord God has given me a well trained tongue, that I may know how to speak to the weary"(50:4). No one spoke the way Jesus did. And he spoke with authority, not the way the Scribes and Pharisees did. He drove out demons with a few words like "Quiet! Come out of him"(Mk 1:25). People were awestruck and said, "What is this? A new teaching with authority. He commands even the unclean spirits and they obey him"(Mk 1:27). He held people spellbound by his preaching. He never used the phrase, thus says the Lord, but I say to you, "Love your enemies, do good to those who hate you, bless those who curse you, pray for those who mistreats you. To the person who strikes you on one cheek, offer the other one as well" (Lk. 6:27-29). Jesus challenges us to the highest kind of love as we have seen, and to speak the way he spoke. I once asked a grade school lad what he would do if someone hit him on the cheek? He responded, "I'd run." The only way someone can strike you on your left cheek is by using the back of his or her hand. This was a worse insult to a Jew.

HOW WE MISUSE OUR GIFT

We can easily misuse our marvelous gift of speech. I often ask people what is the strongest muscle in our bodies? Many reply, the heart. No, the strongest muscle is the tongue. That is what gets us in the most trouble. It has been estimated that the average person speaks enough words during a week to fill a five-hundred page book. St. James tells us that if we do not bridle our tongue we cannot consider ourselves religious. He also states that if we are in control of our tongue, we are in control of our whole body and we are becoming perfect. He compares the tongue to a bit in the horse's mouth which enables us to guide it wherever we want it to go, as to a rudder in a ship which steers it wherever the captain wants it to go. Another image he uses is a small fire which can set a forest ablaze. We know that a tiny spark can start a huge conflagration.

James also states, "No human being can tame the tongue"(3:8). The tongue can be more destructive than a famine or drought. A vicious tongue can eat away at us like a cancer. David stated, "I will watch my ways, lest I sin with my tongue; I will set a curb on my mouth"(Ps. 39:12). Jesus cautioned us, "On the day of judgment people will render an account for every careless word they speak"(Mt. 12 :36). Continuous self control and discipline are needed but not a verbal straightjacket. Our tongue shows the inward condition of our heart. Socrates once told a lad to speak so he could see him. Jesus said, "From the fullness of the heart the mouth speaks"(Mt 12:34). Complaining, comparing and resentment are all actions of the ego which needs to have the last word and is constantly finding fault with others. A cartoon entitled "Egomaniacs Anonymous" depicted five people sitting in a circle and one person points to herself saying, "There is nothing anonymous about me."

Jesus also told us that he is the way, the truth and the life. If we are going to follow his way and receive the life he wants to give us, we have to be honest and truthful, even brutally honest. There is a powerful story told in the Acts about Ananias and Sapphira. It was customary to sell their property and give the proceeds to the church or community. When Peter asked Ananias if he sold his property for a certain amount, Ananias said he did. Actually Ananias sold it for more and wanted to keep some for himself. He was struck dead on the spot. Next, Sapphira comes in and she is asked the same question, and also tells a lie. She also dies. When a teacher was telling this story to a group of small children and had finished the story, one of them raised her hand and said, "If God did that today, there would not be too many people left." Years ago before the advent of the weekly bulletin, one pastor use to tell the people ahead of time what Scripture text he was going to preach on the following Sunday. Imagine what would happen in parishes if people came prepared to hear the Word of God proclaimed. So he told them that he was preaching on the 29th chapter of St. Matthew's Gospel. The following Sunday he asked the people how many had prepared the 29th chapter of St. Matthew's Gospel. Quite a few hands shot up in the congregation. He responded, "I have news for you, there is no 29th chapter of St. Matthew's Gospel. And my sermon today is on lying!"

The ego often urges us to lie, especially to get out of an embarrassing situation. How easily that is done. Or some people will say, "Oh, that is only a little white lie." But it is still a lie, and that is the point. There is something, however, called a mental reservation. For example, when a mother gives birth to a child, that child ordinarily is not a ravishing beauty. So we hardly say to the mother and father, "Cheer up!" "Things will get better." We say, " Oh, isn't she or he lovely?" That is not a lie, but a mental reservation. A famous doctor who delivered many babies during his lifetime would say concerning the child, "Now, **there** is a baby!"

But think of all the lies that are told each day. The ego is busy. Lies told in business deals, family relationships, or in the courtroom, just to mention a few. How often people say in court when asked, "Do you swear to tell the whole truth and nothing but the truth?"And the response is, "I do," only later do we find out that the person perjured himself or herself. A top executive finally admitted to 2,000 stunned business men in San Diego he could not read. His ego would not allow him admit that during all these years he had lied about his ability to read documents and business transactions.

Scott Peck in his book *People of the Lie* describes the evil of lying. He maintains that people often construct many layers of self-deception to avoid the pain of self-examination. And in doing this they succeed in deceiving others because the ego is at work. They really carry on the task of the devil. Jesus never spoke of the devil as a heretic, murderer, thief, but as "the father of lies"(Jn 8:44). Psychologists point out how it is possible to become a pathological liar after telling lie after lie. The worst part is that they have been convinced by the ego they are telling the truth. The harm done to others is incapable of being calculated.

Jesus told us "that the truth will set you free"(Jn 8:32). People who tell lies are not free. They are bound up in their own prisons which are often self inflicted. Pilate asked Jesus when he stood before him during his trial, "What is truth?"(Jn. 18:38) Here was truth itself standing before him, and he didn't even recognize it. Jesus declared, "For this I was born and for this I came into the world, to testify to the truth. Everyone who belongs to the truth listens to my voice"(Jn. 18:37).

Flattery can be a form of lying. Someone can say affectionate and affirming words to us, not because they are true but to manipulate us. The Germans in a bunker with Hitler were flattering him while the Red Army was shelling them a few hundred yards from there. Imagine what would happen if we elected leaders based on their record and not on their flattering speeches. I always tell audiences when I am introduced to a group, and they flatter me by what I have accomplished that, "Flattery will not harm you, unless you inhale it."

OTHER SINS OF THE TONGUE

Another way to misuse one's tongue is the sin of detraction. Detraction means to reveal without necessity a fault committed by another, but which is known to others. The ego convinces us that as long as it is known it is okay. The book of Proverbs speaks of detraction as an abomination (6:19). People who are guilty of detraction usually defend themselves by saying they are telling the truth. Actually it is only half true. Jesus had to contend with this at his trial. Witnesses came forth to testify that he said, "I will destroy this temple made with hands, and within three days I will build another not made with hands"(Mk. 14:58). The people thought that Jesus was referring to their temple which took them over forty years to build. But Jesus was referring to his own body which would be raised up in three days.

If detraction is harmful, slander or backbiting is worse because it violates truth, justice and charity. Backbiting refers to an attack from the rear in the blood sport of bear baiting. The ego helps us to pull someone down, especially anyone who has hurt us. So we talk about these people behind their backs and even take pleasure in doing so. Slander means making known the hidden faults of others, but with the intention of harming someone else's good name. Thomas Aquinas considered it the gravest sin we could commit against our neighbor. We know from the Hebrew Scriptures that God commissioned Moses to lead the Israelite people out into the desert. But they began to murmur and complain against God because of a lack of food. Miriam, the sister of Moses, talked against her brother. God was so displeased that she was afflicted with leprosy. Again, Moses had to intervene for his people and this time for his sister whose leprosy disappeared. Stating that President Obama "hates America, white people, or capitalism," without proof or justifying their source can be vile slander, according to John Kavanaugh, a professor of philosophy at St. Louis University.

The cunning part about slander is that the ego makes sure no one owns it. Slander is like the little stone spoken in the book of Daniel "which was hewn from a mountain without a hand being put to it, struck its iron and tile feet breaking them in pieces"(2: 34). Slander, like that little stone, often comes into being without hands, but every hand is outstretched to give it momentum on its forward course. Meanwhile, everyone disowns the destruction caused to someone whose good name lies in ruin. A good example of this are the campaign ads used against a political foe, or a business competitor. This can become contagious, luring others into their orbit of toxicity or into their rabbit hole of hatred.

A LACK OF CIVILITY

Many of us will agree that some of our conversations are riddled with non-civility, name-calling, character assassination and disrespect. Civility has changed with warp speed. Has bad behavior become the "new normal?" The ego has to gloat when this is done. The worse part is that it is carried on in the name of truth or religion. Some people believe they have a privileged pipeline to God, that they are right and others are wrong. Why have we bracketed respect, forgiveness, kindness and graciousness? We need to fight for truth, because even war has its code of ethics. If we claim that God is on our side as the ego will insist and as some do in war, then we should radiate respect for others, not hatred. Whenever we show disrespect, we fail to grasp how respect and graciousness are nonnegotiable. A college student was expelled some time ago not because of his orthodox beliefs as he maintained, but, as the dean pointed out, because of his lack of courtesy and respect for others. Living in a highly polarized society results in: war, poverty, hunger, injustices, racism, immigration injustices, ecology, just to mention a few. Many of these issues are emotionally charged and easily inflamed by the ego. One thing some have in common is political venom. Isn't it a shame we can't change this into fuel for our cars? Our human family can sometimes behave like a fractious, stubborn toddler.

"Free speech" has attained a new low because of rampant incivility. One culprit is anonymity because then one can say anything and not be accountable. At one time, especially in small communities, everybody knew everyone else and could easily correct some misbehavior. Not anymore. Internet plays a vital role in pornographic material, invective and verbal attacks without any accountability. Consider the smut on blogs that now is considered as commentary. Even with the caution to be respectful, not attack the writer, avoid vulgarities and slurs, the personal attacks and derogatory remarks continue.

In our concern for the world and society, we will find ourselves at odds with others especially concerning thorny issues. But does the issue become more important than being respectful, gracious and kind? Is there too much toxic rancor aroused by the ego? Do we have recourse to disrespect, character assassination, ad hominem arguments and even violence, to win an argument? We don't win our battles by these means, but rather by showing respect, openness, graciousness and forgiveness. Civility is the glue that binds us together, sustaining our humanity. Cardinal Theodore McCarrick , archbishop emeritus of Washington D.C., stated that we have to restore civility to public discourse enabling us to attack problems and not each other.

Dr. Alveda King, a niece of Reverend Martin Luther King Jr., was invited to the White House where a picture of her and President Obama was taken. When Glenn Beck interviewed her on radio, he asked her if she was not giving the wrong message because certain things President Obama was doing would offend her uncle. She responded, "I don't agree with his policies, but how can you pray for a man if you hate him?"

We certainly had our share of haters of former President Bill Clinton and President George W Bush and still do today. Maybe we need to take to heart Alveda King's words which go so contrary to our ego.

Richard Mouw, who is president of Fuller Theological Seminary, has written *Uncommon Decency: Christian Civility in an Uncivil World.* In it he recounts the story of how he was pulling into a parking place at a mall, when he heard an angry blowing of the horn and a woman giving him the finger. Mouw had not seen her and wanted her to know that. When he found her, he apologized for being so thoughtless. She began to cry, telling him how tough a day she was having, but told him never to mind. As she walked away she murmured, "Thank you." Mouw believes that civility is a Christian virtue necessary when we enter into dialogue with others, and to learn from those with whom we disagree, even our fiercest foes.

GOSSIP CAN BE DEVASTATING

Another misuse of our tongue is to delight in repeating derogatory stories or gossip. Some can't kill the gossip like flies before it multiplies. The ego insists that it's too juicy a morsel to keep to ourselves. We will use all types of expressions: "I don't believe this, but did you hear? or I don't believe this, but... John's a nice guy, but..." St. Paul was not afraid to tell the Thessalonians that they were "not keeping themselves busy but minding the business of others"(2 Thes 3:11). The ego can enkindle a burning need for some people to know the latest gossip. Knowing what is going on in a company ranks near the top as being most desirable. People who know what is going on feel important and worthwhile, especially if they know what others do not.

In England there used to be a game called "scandal." People sit in a circle. One person whispers some bit of gossip to the next person, who in turn repeats it to the person next to him or her until the story or gossip reaches the last person. This person would then tell the story. Much to the astonishment of the others, the story had completely changed.

One day a delegation came to the White House to see Abraham Lincoln about one of his appointments. After Lincoln read it, he said to the delegation, "May I do with it what I please?" Certainly, Mr. President, "they replied." He took the paper and threw it in the fireplace where it soon disappeared. Lincoln then said, "Good day, gentlemen!" That is how we should treat gossip. Kill it like flies, before it multiplies. The damage done by lying, detraction, slander and gossip is often irreparable. We have heard the story how one priest demonstrated this one day by taking a feather pillow, ripping it open and spreading the feathers to the wind which scattered them for miles. Then he said to the person, "Go, gather them." "But that is impossible," the person responded." "Well," he responded, "that is what happens when someone's good name is harmed or injured through gossip, detraction or slander."

ANGRY WORDS

We can also misuse our gift of speech by angry words. The first thing we think of when we use the word "anger" is sin. But there is a justified anger. Jesus brought that out many times in the Gospel. Recall the incident when he healed the man with the withered hand. He asked the Pharisees "Is it lawful to do good on the sabbath rather to do evil, to save a life rather than to destroy it?"(Mk. 3:4) They remained silent to his question, and Jesus became angry. Our problem so often is that we get angry at the wrong people or things. Many injustices exist which we are aware of and need to be addressed, yet we often don't speak out. We, too, are silent as Antarctica. At times when we might be silent and absorb the hurt, our ego urges us to lash out in anger. Some people have hair-triggered tempers. At the least provocation they explode like a Mount St. Helena.

They deserve a sign over themselves reading: Danger, high voltage! What turns your crank? Often angry words burn like hot peppers in our mouths.

Some aren't even aware or in contact with all the anger present within them. I remember counseling someone and saying to the person because I detected some anger, "Are you angry?" And the person shot back with an explosive retort: **"I AM NOT ANGRY!"** The person wasn't even aware of all the anger bottled up inside.

In traveling around and coming in contact with many people, I can't help but notice how many people are angry, anger nourished by the ego against God, the Church, the Pope, their Bishop, their pastor or someone else. It reminds me of the story of Jonah who was asked that penetrating question from God, "Have you reason to be angry?"(Jonah 4:4) Jonah does think that he has reason to be angry because of a gourd plant that died. Often the ego urges us to anger over some insignificant things. I remember one parish where a parishioner told me he was angry at the pastor because he painted the church doors red. Isn't Jonah's story our story? We never know if Jonah resolved his anger because the book ends rather abruptly. When I reflect on that, I often wonder how many people remain angry, or worse, die with a lot of unjust anger that they have not let go of giving it over to the healing power of Jesus. The balm of Gilead does heal us.

Anger can be a powerful way the ego helps us to control others by raucous rancor, our moods and actions. Some think that their anger will change things or people, so they get their way. Moses was in deep communion with God on Mt. Sinai, and when he came down he saw them worshiping the golden calf. He was so angry that he crashed the tablets to the ground. Did that change the Israelites? The answer is evident as we read on. People who think that they can change others by temper tantrums are misguided. The opposite usually happens: anger breeds more anger and hostility. We often say things or take cheap shots at each other that we later regret. Some love to strike below the radar screen which can cause a cockpit of conflict.

We need, however, to get our anger out constructively and not suppress or repress it. If we don't, we are bound to suffer from ulcers, high blood pressure, or some other sickness. A doctor one day, after examining a patient, said, "And to whom aren't you speaking now?" He detected something deeper. Often the ego devises ways for the anger to come out indirectly by means of verbal abuse, like cynicism, sarcasm or snide remarks. We have to let others know directly when we are angry with them. What is not talked out, will definitely be acted out.

Anger often leads to profanity. Some get into a habit of using this rather repeatedly. I remember a bumper sticker which read: "God's last name is not damn it!" Going through a park one day, there were two small boys about four years old playing in the sand and using all kinds of profanity. I asked them "Where did you learn that?" They responded, "From my parents." St. Paul encourages us to speak the truth in love. If our tongue is the strongest muscle it often needs the most healing. Nothing is open more by mistake than our mouth.

We need to say the good things about people, things that will really help and encourage them as St. Paul says. Too many people are involved in the demolition business today which the ego will encourage. We have a tremendous power at our disposal by complimenting others, affirming them. We have to ask ourselves, when was the last time I affirmed someone? We are given the choice of being a Mother Teresa or a raging terrorist. We can feel the call to martyrdom or to commit sin. We can feel as noble or idealistic as Don Quixote, or as a mean as a discontented cynic. The ego will always choose the latter. We become our choices. John of the Cross maintained that we grow in our spiritual lives not by rubbing out our faults, but by emphasizing and fanning the flames of our virtues. That will remove any pettiness and narrowness of outlook.

One of the ways to help us say good things about others is to discipline our thoughts. Our thoughts are the springboard of our words and actions. Look at Jesus and how his thoughts were so positive and affirming. He has set us an example of how we are to speak the truth in love, and that truth will make us free, free to serve others and God better. St. Paul sums this up well in his epistle to the Ephesians:"Therefore, putting away falsehood, speak the truth, each one to his neighbor, for we are members of one another. Be angry, but do not sin; do not let the sun set on your anger, and do not leave room for the devil....And do not grieve the holy Spirit of God, with which you were sealed for the day of redemption. All bitterness, fury, anger, shouting and reviling must be removed from you, along with all malice. (And) be kind to one another, compassionate, forgiving one another as God has forgiven you in Christ"(4:25-32).

Have you ever invited a couple for supper and they suddenly begin fighting? As a bystander you might become collateral damage. You are stymied how to handle the situation. You might feel like piloting a helicopter in a hurricane. Couples who have given up hope in repairing a relationship have convinced themselves they tried everything, especially if children are involved. Good relationships are built on healthy and secure attachments where spouses are emotionally responsive. They edge God out of their lives by not accepting each other with the desire to change their less desirable behaviors. Many couples wait too long before seeking professional help, the average being six years according to Brian D. Doss, an assistant professor of psychology at the University of Miami. Waiting too long can be compared to someone breaking a leg and refusing to get help. Hobbling around for months only intensifies the pain which results in swelling, bruising and possible infection. Seeking help immediately can prevent many a break-up, divorce, or distress in many marriages.

We can also misuse our tongue by speaking too much. What

is the saying that a fool's voice is known by a multitude of words. I often ask children in grade school why God gave us two ears and only one mouth. One of them responded, "Because we would look funny with two mouths." The opposite is also true of the silent tongue. We need to speak out at the injustices in our society. Jesus assured us that we will be given the power of the Holy Spirit to witness to him (Acts 1:8).

Indeed we possess a marvelous gift of speech, but one that can be misused or used well to promote justice, peace and love. We upgrade our computers from time to time. We come equipped with a certain operation system which might need upgrading also. According to St. James, the tongue is the most important of all the human organs. "Listen much, speak little," is good advice. We use it to bless and praise God, to compliment and affirm others which is a tremendous power we possess. To discipline one's thoughts and words will always remain a challenge.

SCRIPTURE PASSAGES FOR REFLECTION

"I will watch my ways, lest I sin with my tongue; I will set a curb on my mouth"(Ps 39:2).

"One who guards one's mouth and tongue keeps oneself from troubles"(Prov 21:23).

"No human being can tame the tongue"(Jas 3:8).

"Not keeping themselves busy but minding the business of others"(2 Thes 3:11).

"Have you reason to be angry?"(Jon 4:4)

QUESTIONS TO CONSIDER

1. Do you have a hard time controlling your tongue? If so, why?

2. Are you guilty of the any of the sins of the tongue mentioned above?

3. Do you make any effort to counteract gossip? What is the best way?

4. How do you deal with anger. Do you try to get in contact with its cause?

5.What has helped you to say good things about others, to affirm and compliment them?

CHAPTER SIX
THORNY ISSUES

If there is an area where we need to speak out, it is dealing with the environmental crisis and other lightning rod issues in our society. We can easily edge God out of our lives by not possessing a deep respect for everything God has created. We are united to the cosmos. The ego will oppose our respect and living in solidarity with others. Pope Benedict XVI has called for a worldwide change of mentality regarding the environment. St. Paul insisted that each of us must contribute to the well being of the other and their suffering (I Cor 12:12-31). We have to care for the ecosystem, guaranteeing its survival. We have become a global village through rapid communication of current events and through, economic institutions such as the World Bank, the International Monetary Fund and World Trade Organization. A growing acceptance of green house gases and climate change impresses on us that we share one atmosphere. Actions in one part of the world affect all of us living on this planet. The ease of travel and extensive migration have broken down many cultural barriers and also fostered intermingling of cultures and peoples. The United Nations and other World Courts have addressed the problems we are encountering on a global scale.

How do we address these globalizing tendencies? Peter Senger in *One World: The Ethics of Globalization*, maintains that we need a single world community and a strengthening of global decision making. Delio Ilia, OSF, in *Care for Creation: A Franciscan Spirituality of the Earth*, advocates a "familial or kinship ethic," highlighting our solidarity with all of creation. She offers to the Church and society a new paradigm enabling us to live in one world. A better understanding that our earth is one huge household will enhance our relationship with it in a spirit of awe, respect and frugality, preventing us from edging

God out.

We need to practice environmental justice which unites ecology and social justice. This will highlight the issues of justice and peace guaranteeing individual and people's rights. It will demand fair treatment of all races, cultures and classes while respecting their laws and regulations all of which the ego opposes. When fair treatment is practiced, no group will be exposed to pollution or other environmental dangers. An assault has been made on the poor which is often characterized as a form of environmental racism. Prejudice can be dressed up as principle which the ego does.

The destructive treatment of our planet results in violence, hunger and inequality. The poorest suffer the most, losing their lands which are often turned into dumps caused by rich landowners. The poor are forced to leave their homes because of war, violence, droughts, floods and decertification. They are referred to as "environmental or climate refugees." In Indonesia, a manganese mining company has flattened mountains and forests to make money. The mine owners become rich. People who have lost their lands work in the mine for $2.40 a day. They allow this because of the guarantee of prosperity. They also don't realize the impact a mining industry will have on their lives and the earth. A jobs vs environment battle has emerged in Hurley, Wisconsin, where a 1.5 billion mine is being proposed 20 miles from the city. The mine could influence the natural asset of the region -- its water resources.

The environment and human life are integrally connected. If our ecosytems are not protected and cared for, all human life will continue to deteriorate. Is a justice long deferred a justice denied? We hear much about polluted air. What about "polluted" politicians who find it difficult to escape from their prison of partisanship? We promote dignity by fostering a healthy ecosystem. Our consumerist mentality needs to be more forcefully addressed. Climate change is not only an environmental issue, but a matter of global justice and equality. Disproportion is evident where climate changes affect the poor and vulnerable in developing countries. They suffer most from what they have least caused-- major natural disasters, lack of food, inadequate and safe water supply, plus the resulting health risks. A new study has shown that warming air from climate change speeds ice melting near the poles as well as water warming beneath the ice. Melting ice in Greenland and parts of Antarctica can contribute to the raising of sea levels.

Thomas Friedman maintains that denying climate change is comparable to jumping off an eighty story building and expecting that we can fly. Do we realize that each year we inject into the atmosphere concentrations of carbon dioxide which took the Earth more than 500,000 years to sequester? We can reduce our use of fossil fuels by insulating our homes, turning down the winter thermostat, purchasing local and sustainable grown food and living closer to where we work.

Pope John Paul II demonstrated a concern for environmental issues in his 1990 World Day of Peace Message "Peace with God, the Creator, Peace with all Creation." In 2001 he expanded his message by calling us to an "ecological conversion." He asked us to take a critical look at our lifestyles, emphasizing that the ecological crisis is a moral issue which the ego resists. As Saint Elizabeth Seton has said, we need "to live simply so that others can simply live."[18] Pope Benedict XVI also reminded us that we have to listen more attentively to the Earth's voice or we will destroy its very existence. The ego tries to muffle that voice.

Are we aware that more solar energy hits our earth in one hour than is utilized by our entire energy system in a year? The Great Plains and the East Coast off-shore wind could supply enough energy to take care of our entire country's need. Researchers, like Mark Jacobson and Mark Delucci, have estimated that it is possible to take care of one hundred percent of world energy demand by using only the energy from clean sources by 2050.[19]

THREE R'S OF ECOLOGY

The famous three R's of ecology need to be employed: reduce, reuse, recycle. We must avoid what is superfluous and wasteful while enjoying the simple things of life. We need to study our lifestyle and its impact on our environment, depending on where we live. The ego will divert us from such a study. Water is most necessary and useful for us. It is a human right but also a limited resource. Climate change will influence its availability. Since water is becoming more scarce, we need to reduce its consumption and promote its responsible use. Someone has said that future wars will be waged over water use. Some of it can be reused. Turn off the faucet when not used. Take a shower instead of a bath. Fill the washer with clothes, no half loads. Buy appliances that are energy efficient.

Energy to be available needs large amounts of oil, coal, natural gas burned which causes carbon dioxide emissions into the atmosphere. Nuclear energy is not the solution but solar, wind, water energy could eventually provide all the energy needed. Our consumer nation has become a garbage society and the ego revels in that. The volume continues to grow exponentially. Some is recycled, some burned, and some buried. Incinerators are not the solution because of the toxic residue. We need to enforce the three R's, reduce, reuse the same object many times; recycle cardboard, magazines, plastic.

Some other practical tips are to ask for paper not plastic bags when shopping or bring your
own bag. Don't buy bottled water but install a filter in your home. When buying paper, try to purchase recycled or low chlorine content paper. Use both sides of the paper, reuse

gift wrapping. Recycle and recharge batteries because they can contaminate the environment. Use public transportation as much as possible. Make sure that your trip by car is necessary. Use a bicycle or walk when you can. Ride-share is encouraged. Purchase cars that are fuel efficient. Save gas by not traveling faster than 55. That is challenging! Eat fewer sweets and fatty foods, but concentrate on grains, greens, fruit and natural food. Do not waste it. Choose Fair Trade items even though they are more expensive, enabling you to practice solidarity and justice. We need to understand that our earth is a huge household. Our relationship then is based on reverence, awe and frugality which the ego can't stand. We need to urge alternative forms of energy like wind turbines, solar, bio-mass and geothermal power. Plant a tree or other plants that absorb carbon dioxide and give off oxygen. Make our buildings energy efficient and sustainable. The Racine Wisconsin Dominicans are dedicated to environmental issues with a program called the Racine Dominican Eco-Justice Center, dedicating itself to environmental education and care of the Earth in the context of community, creativity, cultivation and contemplation.

DEVOTING ONESELF TO JUSTICE

Ashley Judd abandoned her successful film career in 2000, devoting herself to social justice. She recounts her story in *All That is Better and Sweet.* Her mother suggested the golden rule to her which became her mantra, despite her traumatic childhood when she was sexually abused. The ego would insist on getting even and holding a grudge. But her mother's suggestion enabled her to bond with the oppressed, because she did not want to become paralyzed with hatred but galvanized into action. She made that choice over and over again. She is an example of how we become our choices. At the University of Kentucky, she led demonstrations against apartheid in South Africa. After college she almost joined the Peace Corps, but instead went for an acting career in Hollywood, where she became one of the paid actresses in *Someone Like You*, which netted her four million dollars.

Population Services International offered her a global ambassador position which she accepted. She traveled extensively to Cambodia, India, Thailand, Rwanda and Kenya, where she encountered slums, refugee camps and hospices. Here in the United States she became an opponent to mountain top removal mining. Her Christian faith urged her to work for social justice considering Jesus as her "favorite radical." She often feels a sense of hopelessness and despair when confronted with the suffering in the Congo, where children are gang raped and discarded, and where people are unable to treat their diseases. Her ego urged her into a sense of hopelessness. What helps her is to stay *in* the moment, which keeps her grounded in her faith.[20]

Like Ashley, we might find it difficult to counteract the ego and not become callous to the violence around us; our rays of hope can become paper thin. Some of these events cannot be reduced to a simple moral calculus. Too often revenge pulses through our numbed psyches which the ego will encourage. Three aspects of our spirituality need to be developed: prayer, justice and a mellow heart. The pendulum of our concern doesn't move by itself, but needs to be pushed. Are we willing to admit that our sincere efforts are not enough at times, but are we ready to keep on trying? Some of us not only want to push the river but own it. We have to resist being comfortable with our uncomfortableness. Some want to mete out justice like a Jack Bauer operative, or a John Wayne cowboy, which the ego encourages, and we need to resist.

Patrick Carolan of Franciscan Action Network attributes his involvement in social justice to his mother. An immigrant from Ireland, possessing only a sixth grade education, he worked in a factory all his life. He insisted all of us are immigrants. The goal of the Network is to share information to various

Franciscan organizations nationwide, helping to transform the world, while caring for our brothers and sisters as Francis of Assisi did. The projects include "Care for Creation," working with the U.S. Conference of Catholic Bishops concerning pro-life and social justice. Another project is to influence Catholic colleges and universities to sell only fair trade products on their campuses. He is willing to challenge others out of "their comfort zone." Carolan insists that we need to come out of our tombs because we are not tomb people. The ego wants to keep us there. Jesus has already rolled away the stone from our tomb. We need to be co-laborers with God who loves justice.

PEOPLE POWER

People power has exerted itself in Tunisia, Egypt, Lebanon, Georgia, Ukraine and other places. It was done by civil resistance, using sit-ins, strikes, boycotts and other acts of disobedience. Is civil resistance a more effective way than violent resistance? Erica Chenoweth who has done a study of these events found that non violent insurgencies are twice as effective as violent ones. She found that non violent insurgencies attract more participants than violent ones because they appeal to a broader section of society. Strikes, boycotts, sit-ins are available to the young and the old, the rich and the poor, or whatever religion one professes. Violent campaigns require one's day-to-day life and much endurance as was true in Libya and Syria.

Large numbers of peaceful people can often neutralize the opposition which the ego will oppose. A good example happened in Tiananmen Square when a man stood alone in front of on-coming tanks clutching only a shopping bag. His bravery unarmed the military the way insurgents could not. Imagine what would have transpired had this man taken a gun out of his shopping bag and fired it. Then the tank drivers would have killed him. The defections from security forces is over half when non violent campaigns are launched or initiated. When people grasp a physical threat to themselves they unite, defending themselves.

The main reason people power succeeds is not because of superiority, but of carefully planned, non violent resistance. Civil disobedience can conquer violent dictatorship as was true in Egypt. Eric Chenoweth maintains "that even in situations where regimes used violence to crack down on resistance campaigns, 46 per cent of non violent campaigns have prevailed, whereas only 20 per cent of violent campaigns succeed against these violently oppressive states."[21] To achieve their goals, non violent resistance is more powerful even against violent dictators or repressive regimes. Gandhi insisted that nonviolence is a powerful weapon of the strong. The ego prefers that we use violence. We have to choose to eradicate poverty or poverty will eradicate us. How often have you heard anyone bring up the topic of poverty during a presidential debate? Our society consists in the have gots and the have nots. We don't have a poverty of jobs but a poverty of affirmation.

WAR

After ten years of wars, more American soldiers have been killed than the 9/11 attack. Over 6,000 have given their lives that we might be free, and that excludes all the Iraq and Afghanistan casualties. Consider the billions and billions (some estimates as high as 900 million) of dollars spent which could have been used for more useful purposes. Has either war made us more safe or secure? Instead, these wars have fanned terrorist hatred against the United States. We will never know how many innocent children and other civilians have been killed by roadside and suicide bombs. In Pakistan and Afghanistan people fear our drone attacks. All major war combatants have innocent blood on their hands. Humanitarian air raids have snuffed out the lives of countless civilians. A large increase of birth defects has occurred in Fallujah, Iraq. Some babies are born without limbs, one with two heads. In a number of areas children are exposed to unexploded ordnance and cluster bombs. The horrors of war are highlighted by My Lai in Vietnam, the torture in Abu Ghraib, the slaughter of a Haditha family in Iraq, and sixteen innocent people in Afghan villages. War feeds the culture of violence and atrocity. Isn't our military establishment a frantic and self-defeating attempt to cover up our nakedness as Adam and Eve did and protect our egos?

War is not the answer but the ego insists it is. War time is no longer temporary as Mary Didziak, a legal historian, points out in *War Time*. We need to find better ways to solve our problems. Non violence and negotiations can end and solve many of the problems. We need to come up with more imaginative ways to these thorny or hot button issues. Most of us ardently support a strong national defense of our country. But we are troubled by Pentagon spending which leads to rampant military waste costing trillions of dollars. When we are trying to pare our budgets, we need to put a wrench to the Pentagon's money spigot.

Congressman Walter B. Jones of North Carolina initially supported the wars in Iraq and Afghanistan. Now he has become an outspoken and courageous critic because he no longer listens to his ego. Jones has sponsored a bill with McGovern for a clear timeline for our withdrawal of troops from Afghanistan. He does not understand why the Church has been so silent about Afghanistan.

What helped change his stance was coming in contact with families who lost loved ones in the wars. He points out how there are 1,400 tribes in Afghanistan and they don't want us there. So many can't be trained to be soldiers and their police officers, because they cannot read, are hooked on drugs, and are undisciplined. He maintains that if we visited Walter Reed

Army Medical Center, we would have exited Afghanistan five years ago. He has seen many soldiers there who possess no body parts below their waists. The cost of their care is astronomical. He points out that fewer than one percent are fighting this war which means that ninety-nine percent are not, but need to get involved in opposing the war. Jones also states that if we believe in the sanctity of life, are not eighteen or nineteen year-old men or women soldiers part of God's plan?

RESPECT AND WELCOME DIVERSITY

If we are to achieve unity, create community, eliminate racism and similar forms of discrimination, we need to respect and welcome diversity. How can differences enrich us not divide us? Why we click with some and clank with others will always remain a mystery. We have learned to stay away from each other: Baptists from Catholics, Arabs from Jews, Muslims from Buddhists, whites from blacks, pro-life from pro-choice. Father Bryan Massingale, an Associate Professor of Theology at Marquette University in Milwaukee, has challenged many groups not to remain in their comfort zones, but to reach out to all ethnic groups. Massive demographic changes are taking place in the United States which are affecting the common good. Our challenge is to affirm diversity if we want to be agents of peace and reconciliation. We need to move from any intolerance or biases to mutual respect which the ego will oppose. Treating people as white, black, Latino, Muslim, homeless, mentally ill, addicted, ex-offender, gay, lesbian, often hinders us from seeing people as unique and real. Stereotyping, which the ego delights in, blocks us from acknowledging others' rights, needs, dignity and potential.

Many of us need to forgive the wrongs done to us in the past. Knowing and accepting people of other races, creeds, cultures, is a step in the right direction. Writing letters to our local newspapers when we see some injustice is commendable.

Teaching others, especially students, about the need for respect and welcoming diversity is of the utmost importance. Dr. Martin Luther King, Jr. was right when he declared that our churches are the most segregated places because only seven and a half percent of churches are racially diverse. Father Massingale points out that our churches cannot be changed by analysis (which often leads to paralysis) and planning alone. Jesus felt the pain and numbing realities of people as he walked with them. His compassion, healing, forgiveness helped them to be more aware of their dignity and goodness. As his disciples we also need to reach out to those struggling with injustice, poverty, hunger and intolerance by bringing them the social healing so needed today. We don't satisfy them with a placebo, or a clearing of our throats and a shuffling of papers. No stone must be left unturned. We need a spirituality that spurs us for systemic change not just helping others to cope.

Karen Armstrong in *Islam* stresses the need for Western people to better understand Islam. She writes, "To cultivate a distorted image of Islam, to view it as inherently the enemy of democracy and decent values, and to revert to the bigoted views of the medieval Crusaders would be a catastrophe. Not only will such an approach antagonize the 1.2 billion Muslims with whom we share the world, but it will also violate the disinterested love of truth and the respect for the sacred rights of others that characterize both Islam and Western society at their best."[22]

Archimedes insisted that if we are going to move the world, we need not only a lever but also a place to stand. We might have many levers of influence, but do we have a solid place to stand? The ego tries to remove the foundations. We need to stand on the solid foundation of Jesus Christ and erect scaffolding that will not easily crumble which the ego hopes does happen. Who is Jesus for us? Someone to be admired? Jesus wants imitation, not admiration. Then we will radiate

Jesus' compassion and love in our faces and actions. Jesus assured us that "I am with you always, until the end of the age" which can also mean that we cannot get rid of him despite the ego's urgings (Mt. 28:20). Social justice will probably always remain an unfinished symphony.

Pope Benedict XVI and many Bishops, especially in Wisconsin, have encouraged Catholics to welcome immigrants and to promote comprehensive immigration reform. Many of these families are vulnerable to exploitation and are cruelly isolated, detained and deported. Immigrants have played a vital role in building our nation. A path of citizenship can be found so they are able to live dignified lives. We need to respect the sanctity of all human life, and remember that all of us are immigrants traveling toward our goal.

What can be done besides this? We need to learn more about this complex problem. How many of us are aware that in the early 20th century there was a *bracero* program which brought many Mexicans to the United States but were treated as slaves? That program edged God out. Maybe we have to look at our sense of power and privilege and how we use it for our own benefit. Some parishes have started discussion groups, while others are vitally involved in this thorny issue. We can become bridge builders, welcoming strangers in our parishes and neighborhoods.

Pope Benedict XVI has also encouraged young people to work for justice and peace in the world. He maintains that the best way to accomplish this task is having a deeper respect for the dignity of every human life, especially their own. Then they become agents of justice and peace. He emphasized how parents need to be "authentic witnesses" by their faith, charity, joy and respect for others. Education begins in the home where family life is often fragmented. The Vicar of Christ appealed to parents to give their children "the most precious of treasures," the gift of their time rather than material things. The ego can be a parasite, sucking away our vital energies and be relentless in its endeavor for us to have more, which becomes an addiction. The Buddhists refer to this as the hungry ghost with an enormous belly, but with a mouth the size of a needle. The false ego strives for attention by the way we dress, the way we behave, the way we relate to others. If we have no center, we are shattered when experiencing a divorce or some other tragic event.

We also need to respect the poor and hungry. One of the most effective ways to counteract poverty and hunger is to voice our opinion with those in power. Keep in mind that we don't have to go to Washington D.C. because there are district offices in our own area. Catholics are too passive in civic affairs in comparison to Protestants who are much more active. Even when we cannot feed twenty or more people, Mother Teresa suggests or encourages us to feed just one. Imagine what would happen if everyone of us did just that. Archbishop Luis Antonio Tagle of Manila is someone who acted. He appealed in a website for donations of $937,000 to feed 40,000 malnourished children. One lady said she would give fifty pesos a week.

SAVAGE CRUELTY

Recently I came across an article entitled "Humankind's Most Savage Cruelty," and wondered what it was. Global slave trade was the answer. Steward Burns tells the story of Aye who was enslaved for ten years working eighteen hours a day, and beat or stabbed when she fell asleep while working. She could not call the police because she did not know how to dial a telephone. Finally, she escaped and told her story to Siddharth Kara who wrote a book about sex Trafficing. Hundreds of thousands of stories could be told including over 300,000 children soldiers fighting in various countries. In the United States, truck stops are the most lucrative places for this vicious trade. Trafficing is a most profitable form of forced prostitution, ending in a death sentence for many because of the end result, HIV infection.

The United States has stepped up its proactive combat to this savage cruelty even though only baby steps have been taken. The ego will make every guise to thwart these efforts. The meager federal resources available often prevent more progress. What is needed is a globalized social movement or what Steward Burns calls a "grassroots democracy," which the ego opposes. Social media like the internet, facebook and twitter can play an important role. Volunteers are needed to act as sponsors of young women and men who have survived servitude. Amnesty International, Mercy Outreach and many other organizations are involved in this important ministry. But probably the best way is helping survivors form their own support groups. Dr. Martin Luther King Jr. claimed that the most flagrant evil is the silence of "good people," which is the work of the ego. All of us need to be involved in abolishing human slavery.[23]

Maybe it is not a form of cruelty but Walmart promises new jobs when it comes into a community. But it displaces many local businesses so one wonders what is the net job gain. Joslyn Williams writes, "One study showed that for every retail job Walmart brought, communities lost 1.4 other jobs." Walmart makes big promises and agreements for worker and community protection, but they renege on them as was true in Chicago, because the promises were not put in writing. Their labor abuses are well known. According to Williams, Walmart claims that their full time workers in any area make an hourly wage of $12.49. An independent market research group found that the average "associate" makes $8.81 per hour, and if they worked 34 hours a week that would still amount to $15,576. Mike Duke, a CEO at Walmart, received 18.7 million during 2010. Where is the justice in that?[24]

HUMOR NEEDED

We are encouraged in Proverbs to have a joyful heart because it is the health of the body (17:22). We certainly need one when dealing with social justice issues. To counteract some of these desperate injustices we need healthy humor. Ecclesiastes tells us, "There is a time to weep and a time to laugh; a time to mourn, and a time to dance"(3:4). Humor, however, can be caustic, sarcastic, hurtful and stressful--all weapons used by the ego. Healthy humor, however, decreases stress, and hearty laughter can exercise our abdominal muscles, lower blood pressure and relax our bodies. We need light hearted humor to put us at ease. Physicians will often use it to put patients at ease. Humor can be used as an educational tool in communication with others and still be thought-provoking. Some people are more inclined to humor because of their background and formative years.

It is related in Thomas Merton's life that his superiors forbade him to write about war and peace. Jim Forest relates that he made an end-run around his censors by using pseudonyms like Marco or Benedict Monk. He had a sense of humor. The Dalai Lama is gifted with a quick wit and humor. He told an interviewer why he had two robes, because even he had to wash his own laundry. When the interviewer commented about his rotund belly, the Dalai Lama responded, "I might be pregnant." The story is told of Oliver Wendell Holmes that he was invited to a party where he happened to be the smallest person there. A friend said to him, "I should think you would feel rather small amongst us big fellows." Holmes replied, "I do. I feel like a dime among pennies."

When delving into difficult justice issues, it is very easy to become overwhelmed and humor gets lost. We can easily edge God out of our lives. Tackling some of the thorny issues will challenge us to keep and improve our sense of humor.

Humor will release much of the tension caused by the serious problems we face. It will enable us to continue this important ministry with a joyful heart and never say, "What can I do?"

SCRIPTURE PASSAGES FOR REFLECTION

"Peace I leave with you, my peace I give you" (Jn 14:27).
"Peace be with you" (Lk 24:36).
"I am with you always until the end of the age" (Mt 28:20).
"If one part suffers, all the parts suffer with it" (I Cor 12:22).
"There is a time to weep and a time to laugh" (Eccl 3:4).

QUESTIONS TO CONSIDER

1. How can you get more involved in justice issues? Has humor helped you with justice issues?
2. Are you involved in the three R's: reduce, reuse, recycle?
3. What can you do to insure a comprehensive immigration reform?
4. How can people power address your local problems in a non violent way?
5, Has humor helped you with justice issues?

CHAPTER SEVEN
WHAT CAN I DO?

This is an expression we hear often or maybe have said it ourselves, "What can I do?" Often our ego will tell us that we cannot do anything, or what's the use, nobody notices; I am only one person and like a piece of sand on the human seashore of life! Another way we edge God out of our lives. We need to look to others, observing what they have accomplished despite the odds, those who are not long on jargon nor short on deliverables. Bobby Henline, a sergeant in the 82nd Airborne, is such an example. He had most of his face burned off in a Humvee which blew up. He survived, but four other paratroopers did not. It is rather shocking to look at him but, as many attest, Bobby is another example of someone who sacrificed his life for our country. He joins many who have returned from Iraq and Afghanistan as amputees and burn victims.

Even though Bobby is not a religious man, he was convinced of doing something with his life. He did not like being stared at, which is true of all of us, so Bobby made a joke of it so he could be more approachable. Henline hoped people would laugh when he said his last tour was a "blast." He decided to take his humor publicly, not knowing how people would react. Bobby started performing standup comedy at Fort Jackson, South Carolina. The amazing part is that in thirty seconds these soldiers were weeping out of control with laughter.[25]

Aki Ra, a ten-year-old child, was taught how to plant some four or five thousand mines in a single month by the Cambodian Khmer. Now at forty some years of age, he hoped to undo what he had done in the past. He was taught to kill, and for three years he planted these land mines, not only for Kymer Rouge but also for the Vietnamese army that ransacked his village. According to some estimates, four to six million land mines were planted during the three decades of conflict.

Some sixty-three thousand soldiers suffered from them and about nineteen thousand were killed. Aki Ra became an expert at clearing land mines, receiving training and accreditation from the United Kingdom in 2005. He worked with the United Nations in this endeavor. In 2008, Aki Ra organized a group of people dedicated to demining, particularly in rural areas, so they were able to farm their lands, build their homes and schools. He believes that he has learned much and desires to do more. Aki Ra is convinced that one mine cleared leads to peace. We might not be able to undo some things in the past, especially those which shamed us. Peter was unable to say that he didn't deny Jesus, but he was able to make up for it after his conversion. Aki Ra is making up for his past by helping people to live without fear and in peace.

HELPING OTHERS THROUGH SCHOOL AND BOOKS

Donna Spiegel was stunned and devastated when she found out that her grandson, Dayton, had been diagnosed with cerebral palsy and would not be able to walk. His insurance allowed him only one visit a week to an occupational therapist. She often left these sessions in tears believing that she was powerless and could not help Dayton. Angry and frustrated, she searched and found what is known as conductive education, a process developed in Europe. It involves hours of daily therapy attempting to connect mind and muscle.

Donna was convinced that Dayton, or any other child like him, would never learn to sit up and feed themselves with a one hour session each week. Golfers or other sport players never succeed with one hour practice each week. Unfortunately, the closest school was located in Michigan, and they lived in Ohio. She decided to start her own school because Donna loved Dayton so much. Spiegel called it the *Conductive Learning Center of Greater Cincinnati,* using the profits from her consignment shops, "Snooty Fox," to build a school. Dozens of people donated their services to paint and wallpaper the school. The results: a child with spina bifida who was told by the doctors would never walk, now races across the floor using canes. Dayton, now seven, was able to take his first steps.

Luis Soriano felt a strong urge to bring reading as a gift to children in Columbia's rural regions. His trips can take up to four hours riding on a burro named Alfa. Soriano is thirty-eight years old, and a primary school teacher who has committed himself to share his love of education every Wednesday and Saturday. He straps his books to a second burro, Beto, and calls his makeshift library, "Bibloburro." Many ridiculed him for his escapades, but the needs of the children fortified him in his resolve. Some children might walk or ride a donkey longer than forty-five minutes to attend his classes. As many as fifty students await his stops to listen and partake in his lessons or to borrow books.

His collection started with seventy books, but now has grown to 4,800 volumes which are stacked from floor to ceiling in his small house. Soriano believes that this project began as a necessity, but now has grown into an obligation and into a custom. A *New York Times* reporter called it an institution. This extraordinary journey continued twice a week for over ten years.

Gabriel Levinson is a bike rider and also loves books. He came up with a bright idea to wed those two passions by collecting books and giving them away as he rode around on his bike. He called it a giveaway library on wheels. In summer he cruises through Chicago's parks and hands out books to passersby, figuring it would be a more convenient way to get people the books as they were walking around. His hope also is that intelligent conversation would follow. Levinson built a tricycle which can carry 200 pounds of books solicited from publishers. As he hands them out, people give him a funny look, but the chitchat which follows is most encouraging to him.

In 2010, Levinson was able to gather $1,400 from fellow

bibliophiles which he uses to purchase books from local bookstores. So the books are paid in full. Often those who take books are inspired to return to the bookstore and start building their own library. Because of the donations he has received, Levinson hopes to give away $10,000 worth of books. He believes it has become a "Chicago thing" and is happy to be at the wheel. Anyone who wants a book is invited to take one, he says.

Evans Wadongo of Kenya, had to share a kerosine lantern with the rest of the family and was often unable to finish his homework. He felt frustrated because he could not compete with the other kids who had lighting. Children often dropped out of school because of this and remain poor the rest of their lives. Wadongo wanted to change this pattern with his project,"Use Solar, Save Lives." While attending Kenya University, he experimented with LED (light-emitting diodes) lighting. It dawned on him that this could be used to light rural homes. It happened that he found a discarded piece of solar paneling which enabled him to light a number of LED's. Thus a project was discovered.

He now designs these solar panels which are called MwangaBora, in Swahili means "good light." The cost of $20 per lantern is covered mainly through donations, and he delivers them for free in rural areas. He believes that these lanterns are helping families to earn a living and sustain themselves. Wadongo refuses to be paid for his work and eats only one meal a day, allowing him to build more lanterns. At the age of twenty-three, his goal is to lift Africa from a dark to a bright continent. Families that once spent money on dangerous kerosene lanterns are using the money to buy food and other essentials.

THE ELDERLY

At times our elderly remain invisible, isolated, ignored by our bustling and active society, abandoned so often in nursing homes. Another way we edge God out of our lives. Irene Zola experienced this one day when her mother was placed in a nursing home after suffering a stroke. She felt upset that we don't have a place for the elderly besides a nursing home. When her friend suggested that people in the area might be able to take care of themselves, she started and became executive director of Morningside Village in a Manhatten neighborhood in 2009. The region is bounded by 110th and 116th Streets between Morningside Drive and Riverside Drive. The elderly are paired with some fifty local volunteers who assist them in their daily needs which might include paying their bills, shopping, or taking them on a stroll. Other tasks are providing transportation to doctor appointments, preparing a meal or doing tasks around the house. Some twenty-seven elders are served and ten of them receive daily visits.

One estimate of people older than sixty-five living alone is forty million. Volunteers are paired with someone more experienced and are trained. They include college graduate students, social workers, doctors and lawyers. Barbara Alper who is making portraits of the elderly, states that we overlook the elderly and don't realize the treasure they are. Morningside Village survives on private donations, and Zola is helping the elderly to "age in place."

Narayanan Krishnan of India, was a chef serving some very wealthy clients and cooking in a five-star hotel. But one day he saw an elderly man eating his own waste for food. That changed his life. He was thoroughly shocked and started to feed this man. Now he daily delivers his homecooked vegetarian meals to about four hundred people, often feeding them himself. These people are mainly nameless and don't know where they came from. Unable to beg or ask for help they truly are destitute, powerless, alone, having been abandoned by their families.

Krishnan seeks them out, having founded a nonprofit organization in 2003 called *Akshaya Trust*. In Sanskrit this means "imperishable," or "undecaying." It signifies that compassion or reaching out to others should never perish or decay. The spirit of helping others must never fail or die out because that is the way we edge God out. Krishnan was deeply touched and responded to a need. He also admits that he receives his energy from the people he feeds.

Chaya Turrow is a gifted UCLA college student who loves karate and has a black belt to prove it, and a snowboarder plus a bass player. She is very confident at nineteen years of age, devoting much of her time helping people who have only days to live. Turrow is a spokesperson for *Our Community House of Hope* (OCHH) raising $108,000 in the Los Angeles area for people at the end of their lives who could not afford help. She believes that people who are terminally ill and about to die should not be concerned about medical bills. Worry should not be part of their lives, she maintains.

Turrow learned about hospice care when she witnessed her parents struggle to take care of her grandmother who was dying. She volunteered her services at the hospice care centers and enlisted her Girl Scouts troop to produce blankets for hospice patients. When the OCHH opens, Turrow plans on being one of the first volunteers. She believes that if we don't help these patients, they certainly will not have the energy or desire to help themselves.

RESPONDING TO NEEDS

Shayne Moore is convinced that all of us can be empowered to change and heal the world. That way we do not edge God out of our lives. Her conversion happened when she attended a concert conducted by Bono at Wheaton College in Wheaton, Illinois, who in a clear, clarion call challenged his audience to take action concerning the suffering in Africa. Soon she found herself attending a meeting at a Franciscan Convent with a group of social activists who were planning to make African

AIDS an issue and a priority. Moore could not deny God's call to get involved in helping the poorest of the poor in the world. God was also calling her to show up for the meetings during the ensuing months, becoming involved in the grassroots organization ONE Campaign which was co-founded by Bono. Since that eventful moment, Shayne Moore has lobbied politicians in Washington, D.C., and traveled a number of times to Africa seeing first hand the ravaged communities there. Moore is now on the board of directors of an AIDS village in Kenya. Bono admonishes politicians to watch out because he states Moore is "an unstoppable force." She is convinced that real change can take place right where we are, and it begins with a compassionate heart, one willing to share with others trying to make the world a better place. Moore writes that she is one woman with one voice, attending one church, but believes that many voices can change the world.

The honeybees in their 2.5 million colonies are in trouble. They are under assault because of pesticides, parasites and poor nutrition. Also, they are being decimated by an incurable malady causing the collapse of their colonies. The domino effect is that so many fruits and vegetables depend on bee pollination. Maria Spivak, an entomologist at the University of Minnesota, has come to their rescue. She found that bees have an innate ability to detect other ailing bees or larvae and kick them out of the hives before they can do any damage to the colony. What she does is to breed the kind of bees which are resistant to any kind of these illnesses.

Spivak travels across our United States teaching beekeepers how to make sure their hives are stronger, but, at the same time, showing them how to produce genetic diversity. She wants to build a different and unique bee research and discovery center where we will be able to watch her research team at work. Her hope is to inspire people so they come away having a concern for bees. She maintains that they are "social, beautiful and humbling."

Drew Johnson, at the age of 30, was becoming restless at

home in Boise, Idaho. So he dreamt a way to get away from his house. His love for travel, public service, and technology urged him to travel around the country doing good works and documenting them on a website. By late 2009, he had gone to forty-eight states in forty-eight weeks volunteering twenty hours a week wherever his services were needed. That included a farm for rescued horses in Glenville, Pennsylvania and a bowling tournament in Omaha, Nebraska.

Often when Johnson showed up at a place, people would say to him that he came at just the right time. He finished all his trips in Wyoming. His volunteer adventures are located on his website with the hope that others will be inspired to get involved in their own communities. He also believes that if one or two persons can be encouraged to do this, they also will receive the same response: you showed up just at the right time.

Most of us have seen or been in contact with what are known as street people. Paul is an example of someone who was once married, raised a family, but now struggles to survive. For breakfast he goes to St. James Episcopal church located on Wisconsin Avenue in Milwaukee, Wisconsin. For lunch he walks to St. John's Cathedral which is followed by another two mile walk to St. Benedict's for supper located on 9th and State. By walking he saves gas and money for job interviews.

While at St. Ben's, Paul asked Brother David Schwab, a Capuchin, what he could do to help because of his expertise is carpentry. The women's restroom had been vandalized, so Brother Dave asked him to repair the damages which gave him a sense of dignity and good will. "He is willing to help us in any way he can to make our world a better place," said Brother Dave. Paul has come to know all the Capuchin friars at St. Ben's, and has found them warm and sincere. He would like to donate more of his time to support the Capuchins at St. Ben's community meal which feeds thousands of people every year.

Carolyn and Kiel Twietmeyer are considered by many as crazy adopting six children from Ethiopia because they have seven biological children. Two of the adopted children have suffered from HIV and AIDS, but they consider this a miracle to have their family enlarged by people across the world. When adopted, nine year Samuel was HIV positive. Selah, who was eleven-years-old, weighed only thirty-two pounds and not expected to live because of AIDS. Carolyn gave her a blood transfusion which enabled Selah to travel to her new home in Joliet, Illinois. Each of these two children had two siblings which added up to six. Carolyn and Kiel could not leave them behind.

The Tietmeyer's launched a program entitled *Project Hopeful,* trying to help parents better understand the blessings of adopting these kind of children. Their goal is to educate and encourage other families to be open to this possibility. Samuel and Selah have dramatically improved. Sam no longer needs medication. Since they are not wealthy, the family relies on Kiel's paintings and decorating skills to eke out a living. The kids sleep in bunk beds in the basement and upstairs. They still have their critics, but respond with Jesus' words, "You are thinking not as God does, but as human beings do"(Matt 16:23).

Antonio Diaz Chacon saw a man forcing a small girl into his van one day. Married and having two children of his own, he felt impelled to follow the van. The frightened driver lost control of it and crashed into a pole escaping into the desert, but was later captured and charged with abduction. Chacon's actions probably saved the girl's life and was honored by the city of Albuquerque, New Mexico, bestowing a reward and declaring an official day for him. Chicon does not speak English, but what made him ever more happy was to receive a thank you letter from the six-year-old girl for risking his own life.

Chicon has lived in the United States for four years and is married to a United States citizen. His attempts, however, to become a legalized citizen were too difficult and expensive so he eventually gave up. Some pundits have reported the story from the residency status rather than from his heroic bravery. Many of Jesus' parables have unlikely people as heroes, people labeled unclean or unworthy. Chicon might be considered one. Wynona Ward was raped by her own father at the age of three, witnessing also countless attacks against her mother and siblings. Learning that her brother was abusing someone in her extended family, she realized something had to be done. She became the first family member to complete college graduating from Vermont law school. Ward founded, *Have Justice Will Travel,* which attempts to end generational cycles of abuse. The organization offers free legal advice especially to rural families in Vermont, which she considers most devastated because they live out in back roads with no access to services. Many do not have telephones or a driver's license, "so we go to them."She maintains that this type of "in home abuse" is common among rural areas. These people accept the abuse as normal and will not speak about it. Over 10,000 have received the services of *Have Justice Will Travel* since 1998. Whenever she becomes discouraged, she thinks of her mother seated at the kitchen table wondering how ten cents would feed her children. She believes that her mother found a way and so will her daughter.

Carolyn LeCroy paid the price of storing her boyfriend's marijuana in her unit, but not knowing how much, she was sentenced for fifty-five years in prison because of the intent to distribute. She was fortunate in spending only fourteen months before being released. Her experience in prison changed her attitude toward inmate mothers. LeCroy had two sons who visited her every week, but many mothers had no one visiting them mainly because they lacked the resources.

When she was paroled and because of her television background, she returned home with a proposal to film messages from prison inmates to their families which were then sent as gifts. It was the first time that some of the children saw their mothers since their arrest. Some of the mothers were able to convey their sorrow concerning the mistakes they made. Over three thousand messages, fifteen minutes in length, entitled *The Messages Project,* have been produced since 1999, from nine prisons in Virginia. Occasionally, LeCroy has been present when the families view their mothers, and has witnessed them touching the television screen.

Leymah Gbowee of Liberia founded an interfaith movement of women. She was instrumental in bringing stability and a female president, Ellen Johnson Sirleaf, to Liberia. Despite all the obstacles she encountered including an abusive husband, witnessing so many being killed, raped, infected with diseases and dehumanized, she brought Christian and Muslim women together for a meeting. Then she told them to write down if they were a lawyer, doctor, market woman, mother and put it in a box which she provided. Once they had done this, she declared that the box was going to be locked away because they were not doctors, lawyers, market women or mothers. She insisted that they were Muslims and Christians, women from Krahn, Loma, Kpelle, or any other tribe, but they were women working for peace.

Leymah Gbowee had lived in fear for many years and seen entire families wiped out. Now she knew that she was not alone and all the pain made her aware of what she was meant to do with her life. She believes that every individual can do something because God created us with something unique to contribute. She tells the story of how her sister took care of her children while she worked. Her kids use to sneak sweets before coming back from school. So her 200 pound sister would kiss the children enabling her to know if they had sweets. That ended the sweets because no one wanted to be kissed by a fat African woman. Her book describing her life is *Mighty Be Our Powers.*[26]

DEALING WITH HATRED

Susan Retick of Needham, Mass., was one of the many people who lost a loved one in the 9/11 tragedy. Her husband,

David, was aboard American Airlines Flight 11 to Los Angeles, when it was highjacked and crashed into the World Trade Center. She, like so many others, had reason to hate and desire revenge. Instead, she has devoted her life to helping widows in Afghanistan where some hijackers are trained. She, along with Patti Quigley who lost her husband on Flight 175, became aware of the struggles Afghan women experienced through the news media. They felt a kinship with them and remembered how people reached out to them in their time of mourning.

An estimated 500,000 women were widowed in Afghanistan, whose faces haunted them. They were instrumental in having people in their neighborhoods send cards, stuffed animals, quilts, gifts and money. The women in Afghanistan had no support, but they had the assistance of the Red Cross, the Salvation Army and their husband's employers. So they began a non profit organization raising thousands of dollars through bike rides and other fund raisers. Retick and Quigley traveled to Kabul to witness the progress these women are making. A documentary "Beyond Belief" chronicling their six-day visit has been made.

Steven McDonald is a New York police officer who was shot in the head by a fifteen-year-old boy. Then he shot him twice more which severed his spinal cord leaving him paralyzed. His body never recovered, but his spirit sprouted wings during his 18 months in the hospital. On the day of his son Connor's baptism, he decided to forgive the boy who shot him. McDonald told people that not to forgive or seek revenge is worse than being shot and paralyzed. He maintained that such a way of acting would have also affected his wife, son and others.

Now he speaks to various youth groups in high schools attempting to help them to develop a spirit of forgiveness and love for others. McDonald did not consider himself a religious person before being shot, but attributes his hospital stay as a grace where he reevaluated his life and became more aware of God's love for him. He believes that God has turned something horrible into something beautiful, the ability to be able to forgive. He refused to edge God out of his life. Whatever hurt or hurts we experience, we are challenged with a choice how to respond. He maintains that loving God and others as well as one's neighbor is the greatest commandment enabling him to forgive the boy who shot him.

Jesus reminds us, "When you give alms do not blow a trumpet before you or let you're your left hand know what your right hand is doing"(Mt 6:2-3). Dr. Constance M. Popp of Alverno College in Milwaukee, Wisconsin, wrote that healing shawls are given out to students who have lost a loved one. These shawls are crocheted anonymously and given out by a counselor to the grieving student. Since the shawls are made in dozens of colors, one student who lost her father immediately picked out a green one. The counselor later related to the maker of the shawl why she picked out the one she crocheted. The grieving girl said that green is a sign of hope and she needed that after her loss. A week later she brought a card to the counselor to give to the woman who made the shawl, and had refused to meet with the girl at the request of the counselor carrying out Jesus' above invitation.

Jesus continues to challenge us at the grassroots level to be a force in the lives of others. The spectrum is also the worldwide arena or our neighbor next door. The needs can be overwhelming, especially as depicted on television and electronic devices. What are we able to do for those so far away? We have seen from some of the above examples what they did. If we are unable to help them, we can always help those close by. A wave of goodness can transform people's lives and even a society. And don't say, "I am too old." Doris "Granny D" Haddock at the age of eighty-nine began a 3,200 mile, 14th month walk across the United States in 1998. Her goal was to raise awareness of the need for campaign finance reform. She did it! St. Paul encourages us to "Owe nothing to anyone, except to love one another"(Rom 13:8). These words pierce the heart of Jesus' teaching. They have the potential to change the world. We spend much time with our own affairs, but how much do we share with others? Our debt of love has to extend first to God, our family, neighbor, coworker, the person who gets on our nerves, victims of natural disasters, homeless and many more. We should never say I cannot do anything, but rather what can I do to make this a better world and society, because we are gifted and have something unique to contribute.

SCRIPTURE PASSAGES FOR REFLECTION

"Jesus appointed seventy-two others whom he sent ahead of him in pairs to every town and place he intended to visit"(Lk 10:).
"The harvest is abundant but the laborers are few" (Lk 10:2)
"Go, therefore, and make disciples of all nations" (Mt 28:19).
"Go, and do likewise" (Lk 10:37).
"The love of Christ impels us" (2 Cor 5:14).
"Owe nothing to anyone, except to love one another" (Rom 13:8).

QUESTIONS TO CONSIDER

1. Of all the examples given, which one inspired you the most and why?
2. Why are you reluctant to get involved in a worthy project?
3. What are the obstacles preventing you?
4. Is it is possible for you to visit a nursing home or homebound people?
5. What are the needs of your respective community and what could you do to alleviate them?
6. If you harbor any dislike of someone or even hatred, how do you counteract that?

CHAPTER EIGHT
WHAT PARALYZES US?

Once we better understand the thorny justice issues we encounter coupled with a negative attitude, "I cannot do anything," we can easily become paralyzed and easily edge God out of our lives. Some years ago I visited a young man in his twenties who dove into a pool not knowing how shallow it was. As a result, he broke his neck and is completely paralyzed from the neck down. I was amazed how well he has adjusted to this accident, because he is unable to walk or function like a young adult his age. His parents, however, found the accident too difficult to accept and are finding it extremely hard to cope with it.

Jesus came in contact with a paralytic brought to him on a mat by four men. This event becomes a turning point in the Gospel of Mark, because Jesus showed that he had power not only to heal physical ills but spiritual as well. He said, "Which is easier, to say to the paralytic, 'Your sins are forgiven,' or to say, 'Rise, pick up your mat and walk?'"(Mk 2:9) It is easier to prove that the man was healed of his paralysis than to prove his sins were forgiven. *Yom Kippur* in Judaism is a "Day of Atonement," where pardon is sought from God for sins committed in the previous year (Lv 23:27). On this day, acts of penance are performed because they believed God forgave them. Jews can confess their sins to a rabbi, but he cannot offer forgiveness because their key belief is that only God can forgive them. The rabbis maintained that no one was healed of sickness unless all one's sins were forgiven. The paralytic was cured, so evidently his sins were forgiven. But for the Jews to forgive someone's sins was blasphemy and that, according to Leviticus, was punishable by stoning the person (24:16). So this incident, even though it confused and baffled the Scribes, gave them an opportunity to accuse Jesus of blasphemy, because they did not accept his divinity. Their ego prevented this from happening.

We need to ask what paralyzes us? Fear does, and our ego will increase it. Many of us fear the sacrament of reconciliation. I heard of a doctor who said that he would rather perform the most delicate operation than to avail himself of this sacrament. Some would rather go to a dentist than to this sacrament. Their fear becomes evident to me when, instead of saying, "Bless me, father, for I have sinned," they utter, "Bless us, O Lord, and these your gifts." Then I know they are nervous and uptight. So I help them to calm down, and assure them reconciliation is not a sacrament of fear but rather one of peace, joy and healing. Many find it much easier to receive Holy Communion than to avail themselves of this sacrament. All kinds of excuses are proffered by our ego why we should not go: too busy, keep putting it off, the times available are not convenient for me, don't have any mortal sins to confess, have the same old sins, don't see the need for it. When speaking about the sacrament at a parish renewal, I offer some examples of what might be considered good encounters with Christ. I also make it very clear that these are *not* actual confessions. We don't sit in the reconciliation rooms and take down the best ones! In some churches a red and green light indicates when someone is present or not. Some times the red light might appear brighter and we react, "He has a hot one in there."

The examples I give are: a wife who found out that her spouse had cheated on her, and how angry she became; a widow who admits she failed to help others worse off than herself and did not vote in the last election which is a sin of omission. I hear many, many sins of commission but very few sins of omission. Yet, how are we going to judged some day? Jesus said, "I was hungry and you gave me no food, I was thirsty and you gave me no drink, a stranger and you gave me no welcome; naked and you gave me no clothing, ill and in prison, and you did not care for me"(Mt 25:42-43). Other examples: a single person who suddenly becomes aware of being a racist. That is a tremendous grace. How many of us can say we are not racists, or don't make derogatory remarks concerning another nationality? Or a teenager who refuses to listen to his parents and continues to get into arguments. Then you have smaller children coming to the sacrament. This happened before face to face confessions were in vogue. The child said, "I committed adultery three times." The priest asked how old the child was. He responded, "Nine years old." "What do you mean you committed adultery three times," the priest asked. He responded, "I committed a sin against an adult three times."

What amazes me is how some are able to remember the exact number of venial sins, four of this, five of those, seven of another kind. I know how I kept track of my sins in a small book when I was in the minor seminary. Every time that I committed a sin, I would enter it. One day I lost the book and one of my buddies found it. As he handed it back to me, he said, "That was interesting reading." Actually all our venial sins are included in every encounter with Christ so we don't need the grocery list approach. Don't we say at the end of our confession, I wish to include all my sins? We have, however, an obligation to confess serious or mortal sins. Bernard of Clairvaux maintained that "There are more people converted from mortal sin to grace, than there are religious converted from good to better."[27]

When encouraged to zoom in on one area that they should work on, penitents make far greater progress. I often ask them at the end of their encounter, what they feel will really help them to be a better Catholic or person. Inevitably, they give me a couple of areas which is encouraged by the ego. So I finally succeed in getting them to name one area, like patience. The ego encourages us to impatience. It is interesting going into the derivation of that word because it comes from a Latin word *patior* which means to suffer. If we are going to be patient with ourselves, because that is the reason we are often impatient with others, we are going to suffer. But the results are worth the effort, especially when we examine the cause of our impatience which usually is our desire for control. We don't realize how much we want to control our lives, the lives of others, and even God.

I try to encourage penitents to go to confession face to face because it is far more personal. The second reason is even more important, because it gives the priest the opportunity to impose hands on them. As we have seen, the power of touch is brought out so forcefully in Jesus' life. I remember one penitent saying to me, "I have not done this before." My response was, "Try it, you might like it." And she did. I respect those who prefer remaining anonymous.

The longer it takes to finally go to the sacrament, the greater the resistance grows. The men who brought the paralytic could have given into their egos and excused themselves for not bringing the paralytic to Jesus because of the crowd. But they persisted and came up with a bright idea, better than Ford's. They lowered the man from the roof in front of Jesus. Keep in mind this was an easier task than it would be today, because the beams were farther apart. I cannot imagine Jesus not having a good belly laugh about their ingenuity, deep faith and persistence.

Reconciliation can help us to face and embrace what we might be running from, especially if we need to forgive someone or even ourselves which the ego will resist. By resisting the forgiveness, we might remain just as paralyzed as the man on the mat. But Jesus is willing to forgive us our sins and asks us to forgive others, to pick up our mat and walk in the peace, joy and healing of this sacrament.

Reconciliation is needed not only for psychological reasons, but also for deeper spiritual problems. People often ask, "Why can't I confess my sins to God which is prompted by the ego? Actually you can, but the Church has always taught the necessity of confessing our sins to a priest. Hans Urs von Balthasar, a Swiss theologian, states that "sin obscures sight." Jesus breathed on the Apostles on Easter Sunday and said, "Receive the Holy Spirit. Whose sins you forgive are forgiven them, and whose sins you retain are retained (Jn 20:22). John states, "If we say, we are without sin, we deceive ourselves, and the truth is not in us"(I Jn 1:8). Our vanity can outrun our sanity which is true of the ego. James not only exhorted Christians to be anointed, but also to have their sins forgiven when he wrote, "If he/she has committed any sins, he/she will be forgiven"(5:15). St. Paul emphasized its importance that God "has reconciled us to himself through Christ and given us the ministry of reconciliation"(2 Cor 5:18). We often forget that we also become reconcilers by being reconciled.

OTHER FEARS CAN PARALYZE US

The Scriptures help us to cope with fear because the phrase "fear not," is repeated at least 365 times in the Scriptures, one for every day of the year. Jesus pointed out how fear is useless, what is needed is greater trust. He often had to remind the Apostles how fearful they were, "Oh, you of little faith"(Mt 8:26). He even tells Paul twice in the Acts, in a personal vision and once through an angel, not to fear. I remember how fearful I was when taking my final oral exam at Marquette University before two of my professors. But once finished, it was another example of how the anticipation is worse than the realization. St. John tells us that "perfect love drives out fear"(I Jn 4:18). If we are able to love God, others and ourselves as perfectly as we can, the ego will not be able to stop the fear from dissipating in our lives as it did in the lives of the saints. Loving ourselves can be more challenging than we realize. Just remember the last time you had your picture taken and you got the pictures back. What was your reaction? Self hatred is more present in our lives than we realize. Yet, what challenges us to accept ourselves is how much God loves us unconditionally despite our faults, shortcomings, imperfections and even our sins. The only thing we can give back to God that we have not received are our sins. So many of God's gifts are left unwrapped which is sad.

The inability to forgive others or ourselves can also paralyze us. The ego tries to keep us frozen in our inability to forgive. Forgiveness is some times considered a quiet miracle because it can be done alone. No one records it on a video or a CD, but it comes from within. Resentment and revenge can clutter our lives leading to anger and hostility. They can block our positive potential and drain our joy and peace. Forgiveness is the key that unlocks the resentment, revenge and hostility. It frees us from the toxic emotions which shackle us to our grudges which the ego delights in. We forgive not to let the other person free, but to let ourselves off the hook which results in new life. It is challenging to say, "I am sorry," "It was my fault," and especially, "How can I make it right?"

We have many giving Christians, but how many are forgiving? Traveling around the country, I find so many good people who generously give to their church, charitable organizations and community projects. But some of these people find it so difficult to forgive others who have hurt them, like people who have gone through a divorce or have been deeply hurt. The saying is: forgiveness is a gift we give to ourselves and reconciliation is a gift we give to someone else. Jesus preached a message of forgiveness by means of parables. The parable of the lost sheep has as its bottom line when Jesus said, "I tell you, in just the same way there will be more joy in heaven over one sinner who repents than over ninety-nine righteous people who have no need of repentance"(Lk. 15:7). How true that is! Some theologians indicate that this divine pattern might be called "the scandal of the particular." What a joy it has been for me to welcome back people who have been away from reconciliation for ten, twenty, thirty, forty years.

Once I had someone who came back after fifty years.

Their egos must shudder when that happens. Some cannot even remember how long it has been. My first response when they tell me is, "Welcome back!"

All of us need to rejoice because we all belong to the body of Christ and if one member suffers, we all suffer, as St. Paul tells us. The same is true of joy. Once we understand this more fully, its impact might change our outlook on life. When we sin, we have to remember that it affects others as well. We have a tendency to forget social sin such as racism. Instead of pointing fingers at others who have committed a crime, we can better understand how evil is also within us to some degree. This is a call to re-evaluate ourselves first, not society or others which the ego refuses to do. What responsibility do we have for the increase of crime or other evils? Self examination is often the beginning of change. We need to look at ourselves to find out how we value people, or how biased we are toward another race, nationality or religion? Are we willing to love others who are different? We might be able to say that we don't kill someone, but how often do we "kill" a person with our thoughts, prejudices and judgments?

If we refuse to forgive, we carry our toxic attitude into our relationships which distorts and darkens our lenses. Hate is the death knell for healing. It results in constant friction, mistrust, acid rancor, self pity and always being right which are the weapons of the ego. Some love to wear know-it-all hats. We keep rehashing the experience over and over which only drives the wedge deeper. Our critical attitude continues to rear its ugly head setting ourselves up as judge and jury.

Jesus used another powerful parable to bring out the forgiveness of our loving God, the prodigal son story. Actually it ought to be called the prodigal father story because the father waits patiently for his return and then takes the initiative to welcome him back. He runs out to greet his son, embraces him, kisses him, kills the fatted calf and has a party. A teacher was one day telling this beautiful story to a group of small children. When she finished, she asked the children, "Whom do you feel sorry for the most in the story?" She hoped that one of them would say the elder son who was so upset. Finally, a hand shot up and the child said, "I feel sorry for the most, the fatted calf." Some years ago I remember seeing a video about a son who got angry with his father and left home. He got involved in drugs, lost his job, slept with the homeless, and, like the prodigal son, finally came to his senses which is one of the key lines in this story. He wrote to his father saying that he was coming back and asked that he leave a light on in the house indicating he was welcomed back. As he neared his home, he asked the man who had picked him up on the highway to see if a light was on because he was afraid. The driver responded, "Look." When he removed his hand from his eyes, the repentant son saw all the lights were on in his father's home. That is our God who forgives us and now asks us to forgive others or ourselves. Richard Rohr maintains "Every time God forgives us, God is saying that God's own rules do not matter as much as the relationship that God wants to create with us."[28] The line concerning the elder son, "he refused to enter the house," indicates how hurts, unjust anger, resentment can paralyze us so that we remain in the grip of the ego.

As a kid I remember we had a sump pump in our basement. I was adjusting something on it when all the electricity shot through my body. I could not let go. I yelled at my brother, "Pull the plug, pull the plug!" He did, which saved me. That image reminds me of people who hang on to their hurts, revenge, resentment or a grudge. They are paralyzed until they let go, or "pull the plug."

Jesus not only preached a message of forgiveness, he put it into action. He forgave Judas who betrayed him for thirty pieces of silver and could call him friend. If we have ever been betrayed by someone, we know how difficult it is to forgive and how easily that relationship can be paralyzed.

This is so true of spouses who cheat on each other. In my own case, I tried helping some people, but they misinterpreted what I was trying to do and turned against me. At those times we need to look to Jesus and see how he handled Judas and could still call him friend.

Peter one day asked Jesus how often he had to forgive, seven times? For a Jew to forgive twice was commendable. So Peter triples the amount and adds one more which is the perfect number in Scripture thinking that ought to do it. Jesus replies, "not seven times but seventy-seven times"(Mt. 18: 22). So does that mean once we reach the perfect number of 490, that's it? No, we have to forgive again, again and again, which is why living our Christianity today is so challenging and the ego does everything to prevent this. How many of us can accept Jesus' challenge? When we do, we prevent ourselves from edging God out of our lives.

Peter found out what it meant to be forgiven by Jesus when he denied him three times. Jesus, however, did not bawl him out saying, "See, I told you this would happen or, Peter, I have had it with you, I am not going to build my church on you. You are finished." No, he gave him a loving glance, and Peter goes away weeping bitterly, the action which changed his life. We need more loving glances rather than angry eyes which the ego supplies. We might have a tendency to say to someone who has made a mistake, "I told you so. Why don't you listen?" Again we need to go to Jesus and learn from him. Solomon did not say "wisdom"when asked what he wanted, as many people believe, but an understanding heart. That means to "stand under" someone and support the person.

We have a choice to either bind up others by refusing to forgive or to free them. Jesus unloosed others like Lazarus, Mary Magdalene, Zacheus and many more. If we continue to bind up people by our refusal to forgive which the ego encourages us to do, the light of Jesus will not shine through us; we don't reveal God's image. Refusing to forgive someone else binds us up, not the other person. In forgiving others or ourselves, which is sometimes harder, we act like Jesus calling forth Lazarus from the tomb and telling the people to untie him. We are free at last!

WHY IS IT HARD TO FORGIVE?

Why is it that we find it so hard at times to forgive? One of the reasons is because the hurt is so deep which can touch off a firestorm of reactions. All kinds of hurts can be part of our life journey. I remember as a grade school kid working for a man who owned a tavern, and I was assigned all the menial tasks like cleaning out the spittoons. He would examine my work at the end of the week and then gave me fifty cents. One time he threw the money on the ground and had me pick it up. I cried all the way home, and it took a long time to shake myself loose from my ego to forgive him and not hold a grudge. Forgiveness replaces retaliation.

As we go through life, there is a tendency to collect these hurts. Some possess a little bag attached to themselves and after each hurt they put it in this bag. Some of us have expandable suitcases weighing us down and making our journey all the more difficult. I remember a man telling me, "Father, I don't have a bag, I have a whole truckload." The longer we hang onto the hurt the more paralyzed we become. I suggest to parishioners, while conducting parish renewals, to put up a huge cross on the night of reconciliation. I invite people to put their greatest hurt on a small slip of paper and pin it to the cross. Then I tell them to let that signify how they are going to give that hurt over to Jesus and let it die. On Thursday evening before Mass begins, we take the slips down from the cross put them in an urn and burn them which signifies how they have let go of their hurts. It becomes a powerful experience for many, and much healing has taken place in their lives. We have to learn how to grease the skids of forgiveness. Did you know that part of Jackie Robinson's contract as a ballplayer was not to complain when people spat on him? That must have been hard on his ego. He was told not to complain, but just keep working hard.

Some of us might recall the story of Corrie ten Boom whose family was sent to a concentration camp in Ravensbruck, in Northern Germany, because of having hid Jews. She was the only survivor. After giving a talk about her experience in Munich, Germany, a man came up to her and asked to shake her hand. She became paralyzed because she recognized him as the guard standing by the shower room at Ravensbruck. Initially her ego took over and she could not extend her hand, but prayed that she might be able to forgive him by reaching out her hand. Finally, she was able to forgive him from her heart. Bonhoeffer maintained that forgiveness is a form of suffering because we are denying ourselves a desire for revenge.

FEAR OF FAILURE

Fear of failure can also paralyze us. Certainly Corrie ten Boom faced this. Our ego will enable us not to fail by our refusal to try anything new. The former is short-lived, but the latter is eternal. One guru maintained that the wind cannot favor your sails until you pick a direction and possess good sea legs. Too often we have failure stored in the attic of our minds. We need to hit our mental reset button and overcome the fear, especially that which is instilled in us by the ego. God says to us after each failure, "How are you going to work with this?" That is our challenge to become our true self. Steve Jobs, despite his many failures, became a highly respected business man, an outstanding leader by forging inspiration and gut instinct into a vision few have achieved. Initially he tried to sell his Apple I, the Lisa and his iMac computer which were failures. Apple shares plummeted drastically. The company lost 247 million in the last quarter of 2000. This was more than of a whiff of disappointment and he could have easily given up. Apple II, however, was a critical success. In November of 2000, Jobs released the iPod and the iPhone. Later it was the iPad and iTunes store which got more than 200 million customers. Jobs was a risk taker and not afraid to fail overcoming his ego because of his tenacity and belief in himself.

Diana Nyad is an excellent long-distance swimmer whose goal in life at the age of 61 was to swim from Havana to Miami, 103 miles. She had to battle three foot waves, threatening sharks and jelly fish who covered her skin with a rash of painful welts. It had been thirty years since her last long distance swim. After swimming for seventeen hours, she felt a sharp pain in her right shoulder and took some Tylenol from the crew who accompanied her. Then asthma set in blocking her airway; next nausea, vomiting and dry heaves. She found it impossible to accept defeat, but after twenty-seven hours she finally had to accept the fact she could not accomplish her dream. Mark Collinger who accompanied her said that it was the most amazing event he ever saw. Nyad admitted that the mind is often stronger than the body, but she still believes her goal can be accomplished.[29]

How often we want to turn back or lose confidence because of failure. Jesus said, "No one who sets a hand to the plow and looks to what was left behind is fit for the kingdom of God"(Lk 9:62). We need to go forward despite the difficulties or obstacles the ego puts in the way. The Holy Spirit will inspire and empower us to move forward like a spiral helping us to grow and wax stronger, knowing that God is with us in each stage of our progress. As Isaiah stated, "They will run and not grow weary, walk and not grow faint"(40:31). Because Clare of Assisi was so spirited, she saw the cross not as a failure but rather a sign of glory. Are we convinced that whatever we suffer here on earth will never outweigh the glory we will experience in heaven? Jesus' leaving his Apostles was not just a departure, but a releasing of the Spirit into the world. As spirited people we are to carry on the work of Jesus Christ in the world today.

In *Mighty Be Our Powers*, Leymah Gbowee tells about the peace talks she and other women from all walks of life organized so they could meet with Liberian leader Charles Taylor and rebel leaders to end the war. They failed, however, until they surrounded the building which housed the talks, refusing anyone to come or go, or have access to food and water until the peace process moved forward. A catalyst was set into motion to end the Liberian war. Another woman is Aung San Suu Kyi of Myanmar who was despised by the military who were determined to "annihilate" her pro-democracy movement. The soldiers locked her in her own home for two decades declaring her political career over. But she remained undaunted, and is now being welcomed into parliament and possibly could win the presidency in 2015.

How do we measure whether someone is a success or failure? Some measure it by recognition, others by how much wealth or possessions the person accumulates, still others by the contribution made to society. It is obvious which really counts. Some people achieve huge success only to lose it all because they have a problem with the ego. Johnny Depp in *Blow* made over a hundred million smuggling drugs only to lose it all.

Dealing with failure can cause stress which paralyzes us, even resulting in burnout. No one is immune from it, regardless of age, gender or job. What we need to avoid is trying to help others while neglecting our own needs. Some people are caught up in the giving, giving syndrome and feel guilty when they stop. God rested on the seventh day. We don't need to do everything and help everyone. We need to develop a method to calm ourselves like spending time in prayer which the ego abhors. Do whatever helps us to calm down and continue doing this daily. Deep breathing can be helpful. Analyze what upsets or motivates us in our job: a toxic boss, gossipy co-workers, deadlines, pay. What will help to counteract them? Work at ninety percent efficiency rather than one hundred and ten. We often need to delegate jobs rather than trying to take care of all of them. We can't be available 24/7 like some stores. We also need to get enough sleep, eat healthy food, exercise every day or as often as possible, all opposite of what the ego wants. If we think we are too busy, try exercising for a few minutes. The benefits will be evident. Share your anxiety with a close and trusted friend, or seek help from a support group.

DEATH A PARALYZER?

What is our greatest fear, what do we fear most? This is a question I often ask of those making a directed retreat with me. Some fear death most, which explains why a number of us find it difficult going to a funeral home or making a will. They find death a reality which they prefer keeping at arm's length and the ego helps them. We tap dance around the topic, skirt it completely or convince ourselves it is reserved for the old and infirm. When someone young dies, we talk about it in hushed tones or wrap ourselves up in a cocoon of disbelief. The thought of death can paralyze us. We die a little each day. We need to incorporate that into our daily lives, seeing life against the horizon of death which is the most climactic moment of our lives. Death can give meaning to our lives so we can live it to the fullest. As the book of Deuteronomy states, "I have set before you life and death--choose life"(30:19). We choose life so we might be able to face death. The ego urges us to get so involved in our daily activities that death is as far removed as outer space. That explains why monks are encouraged to keep the reality constantly before their eyes, and you see some saints pictured with a skull near them. It is told that the poet John Donne slept in a casket to remind himself that he was not immortal. We certainly need not go that far. How many of us are willing to read the obituaries daily as the columnist Laura Schubert does. She believes they are a mortality check, a reminder of our term limits. She writes that it also gives her the kick in the pants to fulfill her potential now, not in the future.

When dying we are mainly passive which is in direct contrast to how active we were. All of us will die whether from old age, disease, or an accident. Did you ever notice that there is no passive voice to dying? It is an activity we have to perform which usually entails some suffering unless there is a sudden death. We are invited to encounter the reality of give and take which the ego will not accept. Our problem is that we want to take more than we want to give. We breathe in and out, and both are needed. If we would only breathe in, we would die rather shortly. That might be the reason we are in trouble not only as individuals but also as a nation. We want to take more than we want to give. We do a lot of taking: a shower, a bath, a walk, a siesta, a car ride. This one-sided taking will hinder us from leading well-balanced lives, and probably have an effect on how we die.

We need to learn how to give of ourselves more to others which the ego resists. This can be challenging for many of us. It can, however, help us to find more balance in our lives and bring us more peace of mind. Giving can also enable us to die more to our selfishness. This daily dying will prepare us for our final dying breath. It is a paradox that we possess only what we give up. Friendships are indeed a treasure, but we have to let go of them especially when a friend dies. Losing a loved one can cast some of us into unfamiliar territory because we are dealing with emotions. Finding our way back takes much prayer, time, and is often an exhausting journey. Parents have to give up their children when they are ready to leave the nest. Mothers cannot hang on to their children who are ready to be born.

Brother David Steindl Rast encourages us to die while we are still alive. Why? Because we don't know how much energy it might take when we are sick, weak and senile. Cynthia Bourgeault poses the timeless question that Jesus asks, "What does it mean to die before you die?"[30] Right before her death, Elizabeth of the Trinity wrote a letter to her superior. One phrase repeated over and over again was, "Let yourself be loved." The emphasis was not on love but on being loved which we sometimes refuse, just like we don't like thinking about death because it is morbid.

Death is not a wall but a door leading to eternal life. It is not a period at the end of a sentence but only a comma. Death is not the last chapter in our book of life, but there is a greater chapter to be written." St. Paul looked upon death as our final victory and stated, "Eye has not seen, and ear has not heard, and what has not entered the human heart, what God has prepared for those who love him"(I Cor 2:9). In one parish I remember a man in his forties who told me when asked the question, "How many of you want to die?" that he was ready to accept death at any time. The reason why was because his wife had died recently and he found it so hard to adjust to being a widower. One of the strongest impulses we have is self preservation. Jesus came into the world in order to die. He showed us his love by dying on a cross. We have come into the world in order to live. Some people progress so well in their spiritual lives that they realize nothing here on this earth will ever satisfy them except God. St. Francis of Assisi prepared himself for that climactic moment and could say on his deathbed, "Welcome, sister death." He knew that he would never be able to unite himself to God perfectly on this earth. That would only come in death.

Death prepares us for decision time, that is how we are present to the *now*. When we die there will not be a past or a future, only the now. Our decision has to be made now to accept death which can be right around the corner. We prepare for what we are to become. We need to die to our childish ways, which the ego opposes, so we can become adults by letting go of our independence which will lead us to interdependence.

David Fleming, S.J., who died of pancreatic cancer considered death a gift from God. Sister Marian Franz, IHM, after struggling many years with imbalance and fatigue, found out that she had multiple sclerosis. Sister Marian also considered it God's gift to her despite her inability to perform ordinary tasks like lifting a casserole. Her illness invited her to a deeper intimacy, a deeper trust, a deeper awareness of God's presence. Terminal cancer patients need to remember the young priest dying of cancer in George Bernanos' *Diary of a Country Curate* who said, "All is gift." Every time we celebrate the Eucharist we renew this reality. Even when Jesus said on the cross, "My God, my God, why have you forsaken me?" biblical scholars point out that this is not meant as abandonment, but a giving over of oneself into God's hands(Mt. 27:46). Truly death is a summation of our lives returning ourselves to God who created us. On October 5, 2011, at the early age of fifty-six, Steve Jobs like Father Fleming, also died of pancreatic cancer. He believed that all fear of failure, embarrassment and pride, collapse in the face of death. You are left with only what is truly important. In facing death you avoid the trap of thinking you have something to lose, a fear which the ego tries to instill in us.

Have we mourned our deaths, losses, hurts, life's unfairness, shattered dreams? It reminds me of a directee who suddenly became aware during her retreat that she had not sufficiently mourned her dad's death. She had to spend time during her retreat addressing that event. As the famous writer Sidney Callahan wrote, "Dying is an arduous venture, for which we need all the help we can get from everyone in heaven and on earth and from anything that can give courage and lift up our hearts."[31]

SCRIPTURE PASSAGES FOR REFLECTION

"They will walk and not grow weary, walk and not grow faint" (Is 40:31).

"Rise, pick up your mat and walk" (Mk 2:9).

"God has reconciled us to himself through Christ and gives us the ministry of reconciliation" (2 Cor 5:18)

"Death is swallowed up in victory. Where, O death, is your victory? Where, O death is your sting?" (I Cor 15: 55).

"Perfect love drives out all fear" (I Jn 4:18).

QUESTIONS TO CONSIDER

1. How can fear paralyze you?

2. What is your greatest fear and how do you counteract it?

3. Do you have a fear of failure or trying something new?

4. Do you find it difficult to forgive yourself or someone who has hurt you?

5. Do you fear death or how do you react when a loved one dies?

CHAPTER NINE
SPIRITED PRAYER

If there is one area where the ego will tempt us it is in prayer, especially so that we do not pray. We have to remember Paul's words, "the Spirit too comes to the aid of our weakness; for we do not know how to pray as we ought, but the Spirit itself intercedes with inexpressible groanings" (Rom 8:26). The Spirit can teach us how to pray as we ought, and not to pray only when we are in some kind of crisis or need. We often commit a diplomatic oversight or a minor hiccup when we don't pray as the Spirit urges us. Without the Spirit, the Bible is dead ink and paper. Over three hundred passages are found there concerning the Spirit, some twenty-nine in Romans alone. The Council Documents contain at least three hundred and twenty references to the Spirit, especially *Perfectae Caritatis*. The primary purpose of the Spirit is to give glory to Christ which prayer does (Jn 16:14).

Paul asks, "Do you not know that your body is a temple of the Holy Spirit?"(I Cor 6:19) We don't realize how important our bodies are especially when we pray. As James Nelson points out in *Intimate Connections*, once I sense the holiness of my own body, I will also respect the holiness of every other body.

The Spirit is alive, moving, stirring and not a tranquilizer when we pray. The Spirit can turn everything upside down, as was evident in Paul's life and many of the saints like Francis of Assisi. Paul was a very spirited preacher which undoubtedly stemmed from his life of prayer. An Anglican Bishop said that "when Paul preached there were riots; when I preach they serve me tea." Events were turned around for Jacob who was chosen rather Esau, Joseph and David rather than their elder brothers, Mary Magdalene who announced Jesus' resurrection, one sheep over ninety-nine others.

The Spirit descended on Gideon who did not consider himself worthy to lead the Israelites against the Medianites; on Saul, David, Simeon, Anna (who never left the temple) John the Baptist. But the most spirited person was Jesus, who was conceived through the power of the Holy Spirit. He was led into the desert or driven out by the Spirit as St. Mark wrote. Jesus showed us that by his prayer and fasting he prepared himself for his encounter with the devil. The devil knew Jesus' strength, but had to find out his weakness, his Achilles heel. Jesus overcame his threefold temptation to bread, power and glory.

We are also led by the Spirit into the desert of our prayer life where we also are tempted. Prayer might reveal to us our demons which the ego tries to cover up: prejudices, biases, blind spots, petty jealousies, just to mention a few. Prayer will enable us to name, claim and especially tame them. But the ego helps us to resist or procrastinate, preventing us from converting, or what Raymond Brown calls *metanoia*, a complete change of heart or way of acting. What we resist will persist. Schillibeeckx maintains that the Holy Spirit makes us aware of this resistance. Too often, as Dorothy Day states, we sit on the fence of compromise which the ego delights in. Or we waffle, are indecisive, are halfhearted in our efforts to pray well. We might be guilty of an unholy trinity of denial, repression and rationalization. We certainly can rationalize our need not to pray or even deny the need at times. The desert experience of prayer can transform contemplatives into prophets, militants into mystics.

As we pray, we need to find out what church we belong to as revealed in the Book of Revelation. If we belong to the church of Laodicea, we read, "Because you are lukewarm, neither hot or cold, I will spit you out of my mouth," we need to convert, counteracting our apathy or inertia(3:16). What a contrast to Stephen who was a man filled with the holy Spirit and not afraid to call the people stiff necked, uncircumcised of heart and ears. He died crying out, "Lord Jesus, receive my spirit" and forgave them for stoning him, "Lord, do not hold this sin against them"(Acts 7:59-60).

BABEL VS PENTECOST

A strong contrast exists between the Tower of Babel and Pentecost. The people were told to disperse and populate the earth. Instead, they edged God out by building a tower resulting in their ability not to understand each other. They could not continue. In contrast, Mary and the Apostles were in the upper room praying for the coming of the Holy Spirit. They were united in faith, heart and mind. But there was something missing in the lives of the Apostles. We would think that once Jesus died on the cross and especially rose from the dead, they would be proclaiming this Good News. Where were they? Fishing and in the upper room behind locked doors for fear of the Jews. St. Thomas Aquinas stated that fear makes cowards of us all.

Once the Holy Spirit descended on them with tongues of fire, what a marvelous change was accomplished. They began to speak in various tongues so that all could understand them in their own language. Ronald Rolheiser believes there are three levels of language: 1) words 2) body-often speaks louder than words 3) Spirit - the deepest, because it transcends words and body- heart to heart intimacy. Now the Apostles are courageous, fearless men becoming more eloquent than a Demosthenes or a Patrick Henry. Over three thousand people converted that day because of a single sermon by Peter. Many preachers wonder if their homilies convert or transform any of their parishioners. The Apostles went forth courageously to light the candles of Christian faith on the altars of the civilized world. Under the inspiration of the Holy Spirit, they were willing to seal their lives with their own blood. Now all the faithful scattered throughout the world are in communion with each other in the Holy Spirit.

Something might be missing in our prayer lives. We become fearful of many things: economy, taxes, bills, mortgages, how to make ends meet, what the future holds. Our lives can become wafer thin. Not that we shouldn't be concerned, but when they dominate or control our prayer lives, we are forgetting the power of the Holy Spirit. When Jesus entered the synagogue to pray and give his first sermon, he was given the scroll of Isaiah. Of all the beautiful passages found there, Jesus chose this one, "The Spirit of the Lord is upon me, because he has anointed me to bring glad tidings to the poor"(Lk 4:18). That same Spirit has anointed us also in our baptism and confirmation to bring glad tidings to the poor. The more we open ourselves in prayer to the Holy Spirit, the more we will be able to speak boldly about social issues confronting our country. We fight for a voice not knowing what our voice might sound like. When the ego tempts us so that we are unable to speak out, we have to remember Jesus' words, "not to worry about how you are to speak or what you are to say. You will be given at that moment what you are to say" (Mt 10:19). Do we believe this? Have we spoken out against some injustice? What we notice is that people who have, like an Oscar Romero and others, fortified themselves through their prayer life.

When the people saw the Apostles speaking in various tongues, they thought they were drunk. But it was too early in the morning. When we are drunk, another force takes over in our lives. So also can the Spirt take over in our lives. Robert Barron maintains that God's word in prayer can change our lives. But the power does not come from us but rather from the Holy Spirit. Once we encounter Christ in prayer like the Magi, we will take a different road, the road less traveled. The Holy Spirit in prayer has the ability to change our hearts from within not from some external force. Jesus never forced anyone to do anything as is evident in his encounter with the rich young man who could not accept his challenge to sell all his possessions and follow him.

Jesus assured us that he would not leave us orphans. He would send a paraclete, an advocate, a helper to strengthen us to what lies ahead, to comfort us in time of trial and disappointment, to inspire us never to give up or throw in the towel. Did you know that Andrew Jackson, Edgar Allan Poe, Leo Tolstoy, Babe Ruth, Louis Armstrong and Nelson Mandela were orphans? Look what they accomplished. In prayer the Holy Spirit will sink deeply into the sinews and the marrow of our bones. We will not sleep walk through life, go through the motions, be like puppets, be embalmed in a tomb, remain in the doldrums of our daydreams as the ego will tempt us, but be wide awake, alert and wide-eyed.

When visiting the catacombs in Rome, you will find the inscription "Live in the Spirit" which the early Christians were encouraged to do. It is also the greeting of the Trappists. Meister Eckhart, a German theologian, exclaimed that we need to put on our dancing shoes for the Spirit is alive and well in our midst. St. Francis of Assisi said that to follow Christ one must be "inwardly cleansed, interiorly enlightened and inflamed by the Holy Spirit." He did not say "filled" but *"inflamed"* like an inner fire propelling us forward. The ego will divert us from this invitation.

STRUGGLE IN PRAYER

When praying, the Holy Spirit will help us to forget ourselves, our plans, projects and problems which the ego helps us to concentrate on. A struggle will ensue. Often we are taken up with ourselves, making us the object of our prayer. We become what we pretend to be, our vain desires, conceited, bordering on narcissism which is encouraged by the ego. Did you ever notice how much we converse with ourselves during the day? Jesus said, "Where your treasure is, there also is your heart"(Mt 6:21). What do we think about most? There is our heart and treasure. Blaise Paschal believed that we lead two lives, one that is true and the other according to other people's opinions or our own. As a result, we don't achieve our true selves which is one of our goals in life. We might have a bucket full of goals and aspirations which are never realized.

People tell me that they find it hard to pray when they are sick. That is understandable because I notice how pain turns me in on myself. So it is harder to pray or reach out to others when in pain as Jesus did while carrying his cross. He said to the women, "Daughters of Jerusalem, do not weep for me; weep instead for yourselves and for your children"(Lk23:28). Struggles, pain and hardships can prune and polish our spiritual lives. It is another way to get in contact with the deepest currents of our hearts leading us on. We will feel the rub of chafe against our stubborn self or ego.

We will struggle in prayer when we forget ourselves and make room for someone greater than ourselves which the ego will resist. In a cryptic statement, Meister Eckhart states that God is greater than God. Our every concept of God will always fall short of who God is. Jacob wrestled (in Hebrew it means embrace) with someone all night and his name was changed to Israel, which means one who strives or wrestles with God. Jesus struggled in the Garden sweating blood because his Father asked him to die for us. He prayed, "Father, if you are willing, take this cup from me; still, not my will but yours be done"(Lk 22:42). Paul struggled when he wrote, "For I do not do what I want, but I do what I hate"(Rom 7:15). Kazantzakis who wrote a life of St. Francis of Assisi stated that there is no better discipline than to struggle.

Our struggle might consist in dryness in prayer where prayer becomes as arid as the Sahara. It can also become bitter and even insipid. So it is very challenging to heed Paul's advice, "to pray always without ceasing"(1 Thes 5:17). We need to understand the context Paul wrote those words. The

Thessalonians were living in stressful times facing intense opposition from Jewish authorities. In fact, Paul had to flee for his own safety. So he addresses this letter to those who were anxious, insecure, worried and tense not knowing what the future might bring. Doesn't that sound familiar? Paul did not want them to quench the Spirit which the ego attempts. We might quench the Spirit by the pressures, concerns, anxieties we experience, caught up in a strangle hold or a vise.

John of the Cross considered dryness as God's language. Central to understanding John's writings is the concept that darkness leads to light, emptiness to fullness, lowliness to rising up. When we experience emptiness at times, recall the time you opened a vacuum packed can of coffee. It made a hissing sound because of the void that needed to be filled. The Holy Spirit fills that void in our lives, so that our prayer can enable us to believe that God is most present when we experience emptiness or dryness. This goes so contrary to what the ego believes. Carlo Careto, a Little Brother of Jesus, maintains that darkness can act as a shadow for our sick eyes. The longing for God's presence is already a sign of the Spirit's presence.

Isn"t it amazing that St. Teresa of Avila spent eighteen years of her life as a lax, tepid religious? Once she turned her life around, she became a dynamic reformer of her community despite all the difficulties she encountered. Her mantra became, "Let nothing disturb you because all things are passing." She maintained that our relationships with others are often a greater indication of our relationship with God. All kinds of relationships exist--long term, short term with their ups and downs. The same is true of prayer with its ups and downs. She also asked a very penetrating question, "Do we seek the God of consolations or the consolations of God in prayer?" Teresa struggled in prayer alternating between despair and rapture.

If anyone struggled in prayer it was Mother Teresa. She admitted that at times everything was icy cold, and at other times she felt like she was in hell. Do you know what she prayed for? That she would not become a Judas. One of her directors told her that her darkness was a means of identifying with the poor. The ego was certainly tempting her. What inspired her most in prayer were the words of Jesus, "I thirst," which she said changed her life, enabling her to accomplish all she did. Despite our struggles in prayer, studies show that people who attend weekly religious services live healthier and longer lives. They are also more optimistic and social minded.

OBSTACLES IN PRAYER

Maybe the greatest enemy to prayer is neglect. That is the slippery slope that many have taken with disastrous results. John of the Cross tells us that what makes us stop praying is boredom, tiredness and no energy. For some it is most challenging to rachet up our energy each day and pray. We need not only a ritual but also discipline to keep us on the right track. Not to pray is a gutter ball decision. The ego prompts us to finish our other tasks first. Besides, there is more aesthetic satisfaction in doing a task or project and witnessing the results than spending time in fruitless prayer. We might even admit that we are too busy to pray because of the siren lure of daily demands in our topsy turvy society. The easiest temptation to overcome is not to pray. If we don't have the time to pray we are too busy, and prayer has not become a priority in our lives. Thoreau wrote that it is not we are too busy, but we need to ask, what are we busy about? We have time to read the paper, go shopping, watch television, work on a computer. Jesus took the time to pray as is brought out in at least fourteen passages in St. Luke's Gospel. Recall how he invited his Apostles to "Come away by yourselves to a deserted place and rest a while. People were coming and going in great numbers, and they had no opportunity even to eat. So they went off in the boat by themselves to a deserted place"(Mk 6:31-32). Doesn't that sound familiar? If Jesus prayed, how much more do we need it in our lives?

We find ourselves involved in a whirlpool of activities. Rollo May believes that activism is a subtle way to run from ourselves which the ego encourages. Thomas Merton maintained that it is an act of violence to ourselves when we are engaged in a frenetic pace trying to satisfy ourselves. All the great saints like Mother Cabrini, Mother Teresa, and many more found time to pray despite hopscotching their way around the world. Cardinal Neuman prayed with a pen in his hand. Thomas More arose at three in the morning and prayed until six.

Many complain about their distractions in prayer. My response is, "Welcome aboard." Prayer is not piecemeal precision. Our minds buzz with plans and replay so many activities and regrets of the past. We often nurture many busy thoughts which churn around in our heads, especially concerning what we need to do, mailing a letter, going to the store, or such like. The ego is busy at work. If only we could airbrush these thoughts from our minds. One way to counteract them is to jot them down on a piece of paper and then move on in your prayer. Another distraction is choosing some scriptural passage and suddenly a recent misunderstanding with a loved one arises. The ego will keep asking us why this happened, who was at fault, preventing us from continuing with the passage. Maybe the Spirit is inviting us to choose another passage which will help us deal with this situation. At other times we might be daydreaming and find ourselves out in right field, wondering how we got there. One of the easiest ways to handle distractions is to pray them. So if we are distracted by a plane overhead, say a prayer for the pilot and passengers that they will arrive safely at their destination. A sense of humor is needed to deal with our distractions which the ego cannot stand. St. Thomas Aquinas wrote that if we go into prayer and happen to fall asleep, that is still considered a good prayer.

Some complain that their prayers are not heard. This

contradicts what Jesus proclaimed, "For everyone who asks, receives; and the one who seeks, finds; and the one who knocks, the door will be opened"(Lk 11:10). Our request might not be answered the way we want it, but it takes much faith to believe the request is answered. The hardest way to pray when asking for a special request is as Jesus prayed in the garden, "Not my will but yours be done"(Lk 23:42). We need to add that to our requests. The secret to prayer (if there is one) is perseverance. The ego will encourage us to give up. We know that Augustine's mother prayed some twenty years before he finally converted. I'll never forget the mother who told me that she prayed forty years before her son converted.

PRAYING OUR EMOTIONS

We can become very emotional when our prayers are not answered. Many shy away from praying their emotions like anger, resentment, jealousy, or sexual feelings. What we resist will persist. Fear will often paralyze us, but we need to remind ourselves that feelings are neither good or bad. They just are. Our response to them is what is most important. Prayer time gives us an opportunity to deal with these feelings. Our fear is that we might be overcome by them and lose control, or that we have to white-knuckle our way through a maze of them. The ego tempts us that way. Fleeing from them is much easier than their having power over us. We are given a choice to repress them or face and embrace them, as the Spirit invites us to do, and thereby help to diminish them. Feelings can pester us like little children wanting something until they get it. The ego tells us not to deal with them because we might discover our dark side which we all possess. Courage is needed to embrace our darkness as well as our bright side. We cannot be truly free unless we accept both. As Jesus told us, "The truth will set you free"(Jn 8:32). It is better to acknowledge the violence within us than to engage in violent acts. It is more profitable to acknowledge our sexual fantasies than to engage in improper sexual acts.

Repressed anger and sexual feelings will be lodged in our subconscious which can cause internal wounding and destruction. We can easily kill our inner life where the Spirit dwells which the ego attempts doing. Sexuality can be a life-giving power when directed properly toward deeper union and new birth. So we need a welcome sign to these and similar feelings into our prayer life which will then result in greater peace, harmony and creative energy in our lives.

We have to better understand how feelings express the movements of the Spirit. They are our true and authentic self, not the false ego which tries to make us think we are someone else. James Martin, S.J. suddenly became aware of his false self as he continued to climb the corporate ladder. Bonnie Consolo, a woman born without arms, does everything with her feet including driving a car. She maintains that we spend most of our lives trying to be someone else. The ego with all its contradictory desires, false moves, flimsy defenses is not reliable, but the inner, true self is as solid as the rock of Gibraltar. Once we permit all our feelings to surface *uncensored* and experience them fully in prayer, we will engage ourselves in the true movements of the Holy Spirit. What results is a calm and peace we all desire. It leads to greater freedom and authenticity. Then we stop spinning our wheels trying to figure out what is happening. Otherwise, we get exhausted in the process and feel like we are on a treadmill getting nowhere. Letting go and facing our feelings, we allow the Spirit to do the work which will reveal to us the truth and wisdom we need to know about ourselves. Losing a loved one can cast us into unfamiliar territory because we are dealing with emotions. Finding our way back takes much prayer, time and often it is an exhausting journey.

MAKING A DIFFERENCE

Our journey in prayer also has to make a difference in our lives. One of the definitions I like about prayer is Kenneth Leech's "To pray is to enter into a relationship with God and to have that relationship make a difference in my life."[32] Why is it that some of us can pray and pray, but little if any change or transformation takes place in our lives? We can still be cranky, irritable, unkind, revengeful, resentful, angry and impatient. We can hold a rosary in one hand and a grudge in the other. St. Paul maintains that when we live by the Spirit the fruits are, "love, joy, peace, patience, kindness, generosity, faithfulness, gentleness, self control"(Gal 5:22).

When we enter deeply into prayer it should enable us to grow spiritually making a difference in our lives. Prayer can nudge us to embrace the fruits of the Spirit that Paul spells out for us. But does it? Maybe we are afraid to open ourselves completely to God and fall in love making God central in our lives. The ego will certainly obstruct this. How intimate are we in our relationship with God in prayer? Do we believe that God accomplishes more in us through the power of the Spirit than we can imagine?(Eph 3:20) Are we fully attuned to the movements of the Spirit within us? Do we try to put our deepening of a relationship on a fast-forward speed and think we have to do it all? Some times the movement of the Spirit is at a standstill; we feel like we are strumming the same chords, or we feel we are on a hamster wheel moving but getting nowhere. We cannot force the change or transformation. Richard Rohr warns or suggests, "Don't push the river."

Prayer's goal is not to experience good feelings or inspiring thoughts, but to change and transform us. Dorothy Soelle, a German liberation theologian, believes that prayer will help us to become egoless, focusing our attention on God and not on ourselves. Letting go of the ego for her means letting go of our strong desire to succeed. Henri Nouwen struggled to find his true self because he realized how attached he was to popularity, attention and success. He identified himself with the elder son as brought out in *The Return of the Prodigal Son* because he had to act like the good son when others were living the high life. The ego convinces us that success is the criterion determining how effective our prayer is. The ego urges us to find out what is wrong with our prayer life rather than to accept the ebb and flow which often characterizes it. The rays of the sun will ripen an apple faster than anything we can do to hurry up the process. We need to depend on the rays of the Spirit to help us to change and transform us. We need to say often, "Into your hands I commend my spirit"(Lk 23:46).

Change and transformation can happen the more open we are in prayer. We block the Spirit by holding onto our absorptions and wanting our way. We need to be attuned to our resistance and hesitations. Henri Nouwen suggested we pray with open not clenched hands. We might be afraid to move on to another form of prayer like contemplation. A good spiritual director can be of immense help in the process of letting go so we can be more open to the Spirit's promptings. We open ourselves by making a conscious effort to be in intimate relationship with God. That has to be our aim. We acknowledge God's presence, but according to St. Theresa of Avila and John of Cross, we don't work at it - the indwelling of the Spirit is there.

We also need to listen more in our prayer. One reason we might not like to listen is because of what we might hear. If we are willing to accept the message, it might mean a change of direction, taking the road less traveled, making a U turn. To listen well we need silence which we might fear or be uncomfortable with. So the ego makes much noise. We often fill our day with conversation, music, texting, work, just to mention a few ways to avoid silence. We can be constantly bombarded by noise. An external silence can aid our inner silence where the Spirit inspires us to overcome any resistance to change our lives.

The Mass can be a powerful aid to transform and change our lives. Scott Hahn in *Lamb's Supper,* shows a fascinating relationship between the Book of Revelation and the Mass. He does this in a scholarly yet clear manner. Too often, however, the Mass becomes routine resulting in lethargy. Spirited singing, well proclaimed scriptures and homilies, are all ways to help us pray better. Reciting the challenging words of the Our Father, "forgive us our trespasses as we forgive those who trespass against us," are definitely difficult to carry out. Jesus reminds us, "If you bring your gift to the altar and there recall that your brother or sister has anything against you, leave your gift there at the altar, go first and be reconciled"(Mt 5:23-24). Imagine what could happen if we heeded Jesus' words.

Prayer will change and transform our lives if we are willing to accept our good qualities as well as our embarrassing traits. When the Spirit helps us to change and transform our lives, we will become better lovers, more compassionate, reaching out generously to those in need, the hungry, the poor, the lonely. We need to let go of any fruits we receive in prayer and willingly share them with others. The disciples on the road to Emmaus wanted Jesus to stay longer, but he sent them on their way to relate to others their marvelous encounter. At the end of Mass we are sent forth to "Go and announce the Gospel of the Lord."

Yes, prayer can change and transform us. It can make a difference in our lives and in the lives of others we touch. The Spirit prompts us to share our love, compassion, goodness and peace. The more we carry out those promptings the less judgmental, impatient, proud, jealous and unkind we will be in our thoughts, words and actions. Throwing one pebble into a pond with its ever widening circle can reach around the world as Dorothy Day maintained. The change and transformation might take time, and we often wish it would speed up. Prayer can become unpleasant, tedious and challenging at times. We need to pray, however, like we need to eat each day to sustain us. We don't need a banquet every day, nor should we expect our prayer to be a banquet every day. But the more we open ourselves to the Spirit, the more energized and strengthened we become. Prayer will keep us growing and make a difference in our lives and the lives of others especially when we are guided by the Spirit. We will become spirited, prayerful, people and never edge God out of our lives.

SCRIPTURAL PASSAGE FOR REFLECTION

"The Spirit too comes to the aid of our weakness; for we do not know how to pray as we ought"(Rom 8:26).
"Not to worry about how you are to speak or what you are to say" (Mt 10:19).
"Where your treasure is, there is your heart" (Mt 6:21).
"Pray always without ceasing" (I Thes 5:17).
"Come away by yourselves and rest a while" (Mk 6:31).
"Not my will but yours be done" (Lk 23:42).

QUESTIONS TO CONSIDER

1. What prevents you from praying when you know you should?
2. How is it possible to pray without ceasing as St. Paul encourages us?
3. How do you react when darkness or spiritual dryness sets into your prayer?
4. What is your greatest obstacle to prayer?
5. Do you find it challenging to pray your feelings?
6. How has prayer made a difference in your life?

ENDNOTES

CHAPTER ONE

1. Cynthia, Bourgealt, *The Wisdom of Jesus*, (Boston, Mass: Shambhala Publications, 2008), 48.

2. Richard, Rohr, *Falling Upward*, (San Francisco, CA: Jossey-Bass, 2011), 130.

3. David, Leipert, *Muslim, Christian and Jew*, (Toronto, Ontario: Faith of Life), 3.

4. David Steindl, Rast, *Common Sense Spirituality, The Essential Wisdom of David Steindl Rast*,
(New York, New York: Crossroad, 2008), 177.

5. Rohr, *Falling Down*, ix.

CHAPTER TWO

6. Rohr, *Falling Down, 46.*

7. Ibid, 48.

8. Ibid, 68.

9. Rast, *Common Sense Spirituality,* 161.

10. Elizabeth, Palmberg, "Faith at the Tipping Point, *(Sojourners,* Vol. 41, No 3, March 2012), 33- 34.

11. John Maxwell, *The Indispensable Qualities of a Leader,* (Nashville, TN: Thomas Nelson, 1999), 77.

CHAPTER THREE

12. Peter John, Cameron, *Mysteries of the Virgin Mary,* (Cincinnati, OH: Servant Books, 2011), 11.

13. Barbara, Taylor, *An Altar in the World,* (New York, N Y, Harper Collins, 2009), 45.

CHAPTER FOUR

14. Robert, Barron, *Catholicism: A Journey to the Heart of Faith,* (New York, N Y, Random House, 2011), 140.

15. Jerome, Kodell, "The Good Fight: How Christians Suffer, Die and Rise with Christ," *(America,* Vol. 204, No 4,

April 25, 2011), 15.

16. Leipert, *Muslim, Christian, Jew,* 154.

17. Robert, Smietana, "Peace Be Upon You," *(Sojourners,* Vol 40, No 9, Sep.-Oct, 2011), 16-22.

CHAPTER SIX

18. Rohr, *Falling Upward, 113.*

19. Lindsay, Moseley "We Have Technology," (*Sojourners,* Vol 40, No 7, July 2011), 10.

20. Jason, Howard, "Where Her Heart Is," *(Sojourners,* Vol. 40, No7, July, 2011), 38-43.

21. Erica, Chenoweth, "People Power," *(Sojourners,* Vol. 40, No 4, May, 2011), 18.

22. Karen, Armstrong, *Islam,* (New York, New York: Random House), 2002, 191.

23. Stewart, Burns, "Humankind's Most Savage Cruelty," *(Sojourners,* Vol 41, No 2, Feb. 2012), 17-20.

24. Joslyn, Williams, "Empty Promises," *(Sojourners, Vol 40, No 8, Aug 2011), 8-9.*

CHAPTER SEVEN

25. These and many of the following examples have been taken from *Connect,* "Stories for Today," by Dr. Constance M Popp, published by Liturgical Publications Inc (LPi), New Berlin, WI.

26. If you want a fuller account of this story, see *Readers Digest,* October 7, 2011, 192 ff.

CHAPTER EIGHT

27. Thomas, Dubay, *Deep Conversion, Deep Prayer,* (San Francisco, CA: Ignatius Press, 2006), 12.

28. Rohr, *Falling Upward,* 56-57.

29. Todd, Pitock, "The Unsinkable Diana," *(Readers Digest,* Nov 2011), 155-161.

30. Rast, *Common Sense Spirituality,* 24.

31. Sidney, Callahan, "The Art of Dying," (*America,* Vol 205, No 13, Oct 31, 2011), 18.

CHAPTER NINE
32. Joyce, Rupp, *Prayer,* (New York, NY: Orbis Press, 2007), 19.

BIBLIOGRAPHY

Armstrong, Karen, *Islam,* (New York, New York: Random House, 2002).

Barbet, Pierre, *Doctor at Calvary,* (New York, New York:, Kennedy, 1953).

Barron, Robert, *Catholicism, A Journey to the Heart of Faith,* (New York, New York: Random House, 2011).

The Strangest Way, Walking the Christian Path, (New York, New York: Orbis Books, 2002).

Bourgeault, Cynthia, *The Wisdom Jesus,* (Boston, Mass: Shambhala Publications, 2008).

Bruteau, Beatrice, *The Grand Option: Personal Transformation and a New Creation,* (South Bend, IN: Notre Dame Press, 2011)

Burns, Steward, "Hunankind's Most Savage Cruelty," *Sojourners*, Vol. 41, No 2, February, 2012.

Cahill, Thomas, "A Matter of Faith," *America,* Vol. 206, No. 5, August 2011.

Callahan, Sidney, "The Art of Dying," *America,* Vol. 205, No. 13, October 31, 2011.

Cameron, Peter John, *Mysteries of the Virgin Mary*, (Cincinnati, OH: Servant Books, 2010).

Chenoweth, Erica, "People Power," *Sojourners,* Vol. 40, No. 5, May, 2011.

Chopra, Deepak, *Jesus: A Story of Enlightenment*, (New York, New York: Harper Collins, 2008).

Crandall, Douglas, *Hope Unseen,* (New York, New York: Howard Books, 2010).

Delio, Elia, *Care for Creation: A Franciscan Spirituality of the Earth,* (Cincinnati, OH: St. Anthony Messenger Press, 2008).

Dubay, Thomas, S.M. *Deep Conversion, Deep Prayer,* (San Francisco, CA: Ignatius Press, 2006).

Ellsberg, Robert, *The Duty of Delight; The Diaries of*

Dorothy Day, (Milwaukee, WI: Marquette University Press, 2011).

Hahn, Scott, *Lamb's Supper,* (New York, New York: Doubleday, 1999).

Hostetler, Jep, "Is Laughter the Best Medicine?"*Sojourners,* Vol. 40, No. 8, August, 2011.

Howard, Jason, "Where Her Heart Is," *Sojourners,* Vol. 40, No. 7, July 2011.

Joslyn, William, "Empty Promises," *Sojourners,* Vol. 40, No 8, August 2011.

Judd, Ashley, *All That is Bitter and Sweet,* (New York, New York: Ballantine Books, 2011).

Keating, Thomas, *Reawakenings,* (New York, New York: Crossroad, 1998).

Kodell, Jerome, "The Good Fight: How Christians Suffer, Die and Rise with Christ, *America,* Vol. 204, No 4, April 25, 2011.

Leach, Michael, *Why Stay Catholic?* (Chicago, IL: Loyola Press, 2011).

Liepert, David, *Muslim, Christian and Jew,* (Toronto, Ontario: Faith of Life Publishing, 20

Malloy, Richard, S.J. "You Are Worthy," *America, Vol. 206, No 4, February 13, 2012.*

Martin, James, S.J. *Between Heaven and Mirth, Why Joy, humor, and Laughter Are at the Heart of the Spiritual Life, (*New York, New York: Harper Collins, 2011*).*

Maxwell, John, *The Indispensable Qualities of a Leader*, (Nashville, TN: Thomas Nelson, 1999).

Mosley, Lindsay, "We Have the Technology," *Sojourners,* Vol. 40, No. 7, July 2011.

Norville, Deborah, *Thank You Power: Making the Science of Gratitude Work for You,* (Nashville, TN: Thomas Nelson, 2007).

Palmberg, Elizabeth, "Faith at the Tipping Point," *Sojourners*, Vol. 41, No 3, March, 2012.

Peck, Scott, *The Road Less Traveled,* New York, New York, Simon and Shuster, 1997.

Pipher, Mary, *The Shelter of Each Other,* (New York, New York: Ballantine Books, 1996).

Pitock, Todd, "The Unsinkable Diana," *Readers Digest,* Nov. 2011.

Rast, David Steindl, *Common Sense Spirituality: The Essential Wisdom Of David Steindl Rast,* (New York, New York: Crossroad, 2008).

Rohr, Richard, *Falling Upward,* (San Francisco, CA: Jossey-Bass, 2011).

Rolheiser, Ronald, *Our Great Act of Fidelity,* (New York, New York: Doubleday, 2011).

Rupp, Joyce, *Prayer,* (New York, New York: Orbis Books, 2007).

Senger, Peter, *The Ethics of Globalization,* second edition, (New Haven and London: Yale University Press, 2004).

Shadle, Matthew, *The Origins of War: A Catholic Perspective,* (Washington, D.C: Georgetown University Press, 2011).

Smietana, Robert, "Peace Be Upon Them," *Sojourners,* Vol. 40, No. 9, Sep-Oct. 2011.

Svoboda, Melannie, SND, *Traits of Healthy Spirituality,* (New London, CT: Twenty-Third Publications, 2008.

Taylor, Barbara, *An Altar in the World,* (New York, New York: Harper Collins, 2009).

Weigel, George, *The Cube and the Cathedral,* (New York, New York: Basic Books, 2005).

Wells, Kevin, *Burst: A Story of God's Grace When Life Falls Apart,* (Cincinnati, OH: St. Anthony Messenger, 2011).

Williams, Joslyn, "Empty Promises," *Sojourners,* Vol 40, No 8, Aug 2011.